Beyond Your Successful Startup

Building a Business

Best of Luck Jan! Tom

By Tom Larsen
© 2017

Table of Contents

Your Path to Sales
Your Path to Consumers
Operationally & Financially Speaking

Creating and Navigating Growth

Effective and Efficient Time Savers

About the Author

Introduction

This book is not for everyone. It is only for people who actually want to grow themselves or their business, to expand their capabilities and become stronger, to find their next level. I believe people learn best who have experiences. When I first realized that every step has positives AND negatives, I became a choice maker. I believe people who consciously and conscientiously make their own choices, in the fullest light they can, then step to the next level. To create one's unique future is to do everything possible to make enlightened decisions as often as possible. That is, after all, the definition of enlighten, to illuminate the subject.

I rarely tell people how to run their business when I am being consulted for insight (not advice). I prefer to assist people to understand options from which they can choose based on the outcomes the options are likely to create. I can tell someone how something is done, but, that does not embed a thought process from which to learn and adapt. Life is not a series of grammar school memorizations and testing. It can be, but, to be continually growing, it is more valuable to develop ways of thinking. It is a mental discipline that makes the artist successful. Great artists can "see" beyond the talent they have created in their craft, into what might be if they execute their craft in a certain way.

Every strategy and tactic, every effort has a cost in execution time and money. Literally every day another calendar day goes by. When the time, money and consumption of calendar for the effort balances with the value and intended outcome, engagement makes sense. When it does not, further engagement is a waste after which frustration and disappointment ensue.

It is this awareness that is crucial in navigating what I call the art of managing a growth effort. It takes far less resources to simply do more of the same to create organic growth results. There is little in that effort except what is currently being done, offered through the incremental new outlet.

The far more difficult challenge is that of adding a new range of products or services, to insert into a new channel of distribution or a capabilities array; to leap into the abyss of invested time and money for a less predictable outcome of growth than the organic kind. The landscape is so fluid and the competition so prevalent, it is impossible to think that any one decision, any one execution or any one method can provide the exact same outcome as 2 years ago or that it will be effective 2 years from now.

There are better locations and poorer locations. There is better timing and poorer timing. There is better message and poorer message. All of these will affect an outcome. Yesterday's success may be tomorrow's failure. Yesterday's top brand (Kodak) is tomorrow's obsolete category (35mm film). Being able to look down the road and beyond the horizon has never been more important. The horizon has never been closer.

It is for those of you that get this concept that I have written these subjects. They will all be just as useful tomorrow and next year and next decade because they all deal with fundamental principals in how to approach the choice process. After all, in the end, the only IP (intellectual property) you truly own is your own intellectual capability. Everything else you create, starts there.

It is with that awareness that I invite you to read the subjects in this book that you find most interesting or the most timely to your circumstances today. Pick one and read it. Tomorrow, pick another. You have an 80 day course in this book. I'm sure there are concepts with which you will agree and others you will not. I am certain you will find a number of things that make you think in a way you have not in the past. Fundamentally, having a disciplined, methodical approach to decision making saves time and money and generally gets the best results. Luck doesn't hurt either.

In the end what we want from an education, or from good art, is for it to make us see something in a way we may not have seen it before. And, in my opinion, therein lies the beginning of growth. It is my sincerest wish that by reading this book you will grow by leaps and bounds, not just while you read the book, but, for the remainder of your life.

Fiat Lux,

Tom

Dedication

An enormous thank you to Debbie Williams, my partner, confidant and my wife. Her inspiration and brainpower are an ongoing fuel for everything I do.

Who are You and what do You want?

1. What is it exactly you want?

Unbelievably, I run into all kinds of owners who have new and existing businesses who have no tangible goals. Success and failure are completely undefined. Monthly, quarterly, any metrics, any goals near or distant, are completely non-existent.

As a result of this, I often ask myself how do they know that whatever it is they are doing is actually working or not? How will they know if they are making progress or not? How can they be excited about the success or disappointed in the failure? How do they align their work toward what they want if they don't know what they want?

The measure of how badly you want something, in my opinion, starts with actually identifying what it is you want. Why did you start your business? To make a money? How much? When? Defined by what? A salary? Profits? Sales? Work for yourself? Be independent? Control your future? Have more time off?

Until you define what you want, you are incredibly unlikely to actually get it, which will leave you feeling like you are struggling. If you don't define winning, you will always be losing?

Whenever possible, I always prefer to have lots of defined wants (goals), like a dashboard. Total active accounts. Number of sales people. Monthly/quarterly revenues. Quarterly operating margin. Products in development. Conversations with non-US distributors. Active conversations with prospects on my target list. Visits to the website. Personal income. Vacations. I want to create lots of ways to look at the progress I am making.

The more things you set goals to achieve, the more ways you can succeed. Of course, you might fail too, but, I would far rather be accountable to myself for both the successes and the failures than wandering around with no idea how I am doing against what I want out of life through my business. The calendar keeps turning. I don't want to look back at time I squandered wandering around aimlessly making progress toward nothing because I chose not to define.

In my experience, those that define the future they want to achieve are far more likely to achieve that future than those who do not.

2. It's about Why

When I was really young, my family would tease me about my constant questioning about why. Whether it was why are there clouds or why do I have to read this book or why are some people so mean, it never stopped. As I got older, I began to develop a starting point for every effort I made, task I took on or project I approached of "why am I doing this". It became second nature by the time I was in college and from then on. Why are we in this business? Why am I spending time with these people? Why are we having difficulties here? Why are we introducing these new products? Why is product selling well here and not there?

It became liberating and motivating to always know the why prior to taking on the effort of the how, because I found that if the why was not compelling, the how does not matter and can be abandoned.

With Independence Day one could look at the "why" of Independence in 1776. The Revolutionary War was an unfortunate how of that deeply seated why; the desire of a large portion of people at the time to write their own course for their future. Without the why, that particular how would have been very difficult to support.

I find Independence Day the perfect time to step back from my Hows and really understand the why for as much of what I do as possible. If you want to improve your outcomes, which most of us do, you need to understand why first, and then how. Without the why, the extra effort required to create momentum to reach a new destination is likely to fall back to the default answer of "why bother".

I encourage all around me to first seek that spot in themselves that will motivate them to continually explore what is just beyond possible for them, and always, it starts with why. With a great why, anything is possible. Without it, it's all just work. Champions do not come from those who show up for work to simply meet the call of how. Champions collectively subscribe to why.

Over the upcoming Holiday weekend, if you have not already done so deliberately, I suggest you get a bunch of really good whys for yourself, and back them up with a bunch of other whys behind them. Before you know it, the hows will lay themselves out for you in such a way that what once appeared daunting, is doable. If that does not sound like a worthwhile endeavor, I would be inclined to ask "why not"?

3. School is easy – Building a business is hard

When you were in school, whether you recognized it or not, your entire world was prepared for you. Before each term, you knew where to go, when to show up and the reading material you would need. You knew the mid-term and final schedule. You knew the class times. You likely got good at budgeting your time to effectively get a good outcome measured by getting a good grade. You spent 15-20 years in school getting good at achieving your good outcome in 5 or 6 subjects at a time regardless of the courses. You were focused and disciplined by the system that was created for you to succeed.

Your consumer product business is nothing like school. Running your business REQUIRES you to create your own calendar, choose the location(s), develop the curriculum, create or select all the other materials, plan all the field trips. It REQUIRES you to work on lots of courses at the same time with differing schedules. And most importantly it REQUIRES you to define what constitutes your good outcome.

Just because you got good outcomes in school has NOTHING to do with whether you will be able to easily or even successfully build a business from scratch. Franchises are far more likely to succeed because they have an imposed structure. Your business is not a franchise.

The successful business builder realizes they are the teachers, the students, the administrators, the entire staff, all at the same time. Each day the business owner is looked to by the entire organization, internal and external, to set the agenda and keep it moving on to the next milestone.

That's nothing like school. Staying focused and disciplined is the hardest thing to achieve in the chaos of business building. Lack of focus and discipline is why far greater than 50% of businesses fail within 5 years. High School dropout rates are 8% and college success rates at top tier universities are 90%. School was easy, building a business is hard. Knowing you are writing the entire script is the first step to making it easier. Now, get others to help you in whatever ways you need.

4. Business is just like football – It takes execution and great leadership

It's College Football Season. You want to know the "secret" behind winning a championship?

If you're at all familiar with football, there are 11 guys on the field for each team who need to make all the right decsions in each given play, with someone directly opposing them trying to prevent it. It requires athleticism, endurance and lots and lots of decision making in changing conditions.

So, how do you win a championship in football? There are approximately 80 offensive plays in a modern speed game. Over the course of a game the 11 guys on offense need to make better decisions than the 11 other guys on defense and execute them well. That is a total of 880 decisions to be made on offense and defense. Therefore a game is 1760 decisions, by each team, ON the field. Combine that with all the decisions by coaches and staff on the sidelines, etc., and you're way over 2000 decisions per game. Really multiple thousands of decisions per game.

So to win the game, you need to make good decisions (better than the competition), execute them flawlessly and not poop out in the fourth quarter. No problem, that wins one game.

Keep in mind, any really bad decision or failure to execute could cost you any game along the way. One guy, losing focus for only 3 seconds costs your team a touchdown that eventually proves the difference in winning and losing.

Football has a new "test" every week for every team. Next week, do it again. The week after, do it again.

To win that National Championship, the team needs to typically win 12 games, or to quantify, needs to make 24,000 individual decisions each of which is not necessarily life and death by itself, but, 1 loss of focus can cost you any game. Any loss can cost you the opportunity to win the championship.

High stakes indeed, but, that's how you win a championship.

To create this incredible mix requires leadership of the highest caliber, also making hundreds, maybe thousands of top flight decisions, day in, day out. What to practice. Who to play. Who to sit out. How to ensure endurance. It goes on and on. And don't forget the media and fans wanting to jump in and ask a zillion questions all the time.

Where is your leadership creating the level of execution in athleticism and endurance in your business? Are you associated with the top people? Are you at the top of your game at each of your presentations or shows, everyday, all day, until the very end? Do you make decisions to outwit the competition or make the lives of your Customers, Staff or Vendors easier all the time? Do you make decsions every day that put people in a better position to succeed than they were in the day before?

Want to compete for championships? You need to raise your game, every week! It takes great leadership to raise an entire organization's game. Mediocre leadership achieves some wins and some missed opportunities. The sum of 1,000s of best decisions is the ongoing challenge. You can do it. First you have to choose to do it, commit to do it and then………..just do it, every day.

5. Consider these 6 questions all the time

Even as a kid in high school, I made different choices than most. Rather than taking traditional English classes of reading literature and writing book reports, which for me was excruciating at the time, I chose instead a journalism class for two years. Through that process, I learned an invaluable way of looking at just about all of life through the 6 questions that must be answered in any news story – Who, What, When, Where, Why and How. This has become a fundamental process that I use to evaluate all kinds of situations and decisions.

As you look at a circumstance inside your business, or particularly when considering any type of decision, take your subject through this simple exercise, preferably on paper (or a document) and you will always be rewarded with an enhanced level of clarity. It can look like this;

What – Find new retailers by doing a Trade Show.

Why – My products are being purchased by people who attend this show already. Therefore, the show likely attracts others that would be buyers for my products as well.

Who – 40% of the attendees at this show are the people who are buyers of my product and carry the category in their store.

When – April for 3 days with setup and breakdown on the front and back

Where – Dallas.

How – Setup a booth and talk to passersby in the aisle.

On the business side, there are two additional variables that I always add. They are: AT WHAT COST and FOR WHAT EXPECTED RESULT.

In the news business, at what cost is a personal evaluation that is never covered except in the op-ed pages. But, in your business, at what cost is actually paid for out of your finances or your time, therefore it is very personal. At what cost is actually a big part of the What question. The real answer to what is Do a trade show that will cost in total $5k (booth space, fixturing, on site needs, hotel, travel, etc.), 5 consecutive days of my time out of town and 30 hours of personal preparations.

Beyond at what cost, the other variable extends the Why question; for what expected result. In the example it might be to write orders with 20 new retailers. It might be to meet 50 new buyers. It might be to return with $50k in sales. It might be many things.

The comparison of the two added corollaries at what cost and for what expected result is the essence of a cost-benefit analysis. If you don't like the outcome of the cost vs. the benefit, then revisit the why or the how and do what might be necessary to change the outcome. (BTW, if all you plan to do is show up at a trade show, that's grossly short of making a trade show Cost Effective. There is another post about that topic.)

Every situation that I discuss with our clients starts with a firm awareness of "why". If you don't have why, don't bother with the rest. Too many entrepreneurs jump at How without actually working through this exercise. Before you know it, all their capital is gone. Many others simply do the same things over and over, year in and year out waiting for the "big one" to come along, never really getting to the Why or the revisit of the What.

Embracing this process can provide you and your team with a framework for lots of conversations. It's simple and easy to understand. And it does not require any special training, only your insight, which is what a business needs to continually pursue.

6. Confidence comes from practice

I read a lot about confidence and how to get it these days. Many people believe that some have it and some don't. Others believe you can study it to develop it in yourself. Still another group is convinced they don't have it and never will. And yet, it seems so clear to me. Why does everyone make it so hard?

We all were incompetent at things in our early life. We didn't know how to hold a fork. Couldn't write. Couldn't read. Couldn't tie our shoes. Couldn't drive a car. We developed experience through practice.

With our experience we became confident in our ability to perform these life altering capabilities.

But, what of being able to talk to a stranger? What about public speaking? How about singing in front of a group? Whatever it is that challenges one's confidence, 99 times out of a hundred, the person has not practiced it very much, in real life or in a closet.

Elite athletes practice every day. Musicians practice every day. Why? Because it is through the act of practicing that the difficult becomes easy. We forget how we struggled to ride a bike. We forget how nervous we were when we first drove a lethal weapon through the streets of our home town. Yet, as we rode or drove more and more, our confidence levels increased.

A corollary to the challenge is that through practice, the likelihood of failure decreases. The anxiety created by the thought of failure prohibits us, as adults, from many, many things. "What's the worst that could happen?" Through practice of speaking to people at the store, on the bus, at the airport, in the waiting area, you can develop confidence talking to people spontaneously. Through speaking to your family, at a party, at a wedding, at the local school, you can develop confidence about public speaking.

If you want to be good at something and have confidence in your capability, you have to DO IT and you have to do it a lot. Do it where it's safe first. Do it where you have nothing to lose. Continue to grow and so will your confidence.

Next time you watch someone who exudes confidence, ask yourself just how long they might have been developing that confidence. How many times has the lawyer spoken in a courtroom? How many times has the athlete practiced their moment? Then, become determined to get there yourself in whatever it is in which you think you lack confidence. Do it 100 times. Do it 1000 times. It's your investment in your future with the most precious thing you own, your time.

7. Defining discipline

January is the largest membership growth month for gyms. Nationwide, people have made resolutions to lose weight and/or get in shape and in January they take their first steps. The New Year Resolution.

To achieve their goal of weight loss or getting in shape, people start up in great earnest making the time available to workout or shop differently. By February, 80% of them are gone from the gyms having allowed their comfort zone to overtake their stated goals.

Why is that? Discipline. Weight loss requires burning more calories or consuming less calories or both over an extended period of time. It requires a change in mind set so that the habits of the past are broken and the habits of the future are embedded. That takes real psychological effort, which statistically anyway, at least 80% of the new gym members are just not ready to confront – themselves.

One week into a new plan (like this year's business) is the first big test for a business owner committed to changing the direction of their business. If you have a plan, it defines the shiny object distractions, clarifies where you will invest your time and your money and holds you accountable for results in timeframes to challenge the voracity of the plan or achieve the results.

Most people fall back into whatever their old practices were, still thinking the tangential opportunity is worth the time to pursue it, thinking that 20 likes equals revenue, etc.

One of the hardest things to do in your new plan is to stick to it and let it play out some. Challenge yourself to hold fast no matter what for 90 days on any plan. Trust the thoughtful method you used to create the plan. The sooner you fall back into old habits and perspectives, the more quickly your results this year will look just like your results last year. If you want different results, do things differently. Being disciplined is the only way to lose weight or get in shape and it's the only way to grow your business.

8. Developing a trustworthy gut

Going with your "gut" is often one of the best choices you can make as a business owner. However, developing a strong "core" (to use the fitness term for the area in your mid-section, your gut) is the precursor to having a gut that is trustworthy. How do you do that?

At the core, going with your gut is a term to define a decision making conclusion. Therefore, teaching yourself how to thoroughly evaluate a decision is the fitness equivalent of developing a strong core.

Decisions are not black and white. Outcomes are not clear and often have multiple variables. Should we do this show, should we spend on this effort, how much can we …….., the list is endless.

What I did to develop a strong core and a gut that I could trust was simple. When confronted with a decision that was not clear-cut, I used a sheet of paper (yes, use paper) and wrote down all the different options for the decision. Sometimes that was yes/no, go/no go. Sometimes it was how much money. Sometimes it was both. Sometimes it was something else. On the sheet of paper, I would then start a pros and cons list for each possible decision. If yes, then all these things will or might happen. If no, then all these things will or might happen. The end decision is typically a blend of a number of different choices.

After creating what I thought was a pretty good checklist, I weighed the different choices accordingly and made my decision. I then put the sheet of paper in a folder (I actually had a notebook). Every 3 months or so I would revisit my decision sheets and I would evaluate the actual outcomes against the expectations. I would learn from the review what turned out as I expected or not and how successful I had been at anticipating outcomes.

Through this process I trained myself to be a comprehensive thinker. No decision happens in a vacuum. Not spending has positive as well as negative ramifications. Spending has negative as well as positive ramifications. And almost no decisions have guaranteed outcomes.

Keep score, measure progress, adapt accordingly. We are our own coaches (unless you hire one). Taking action, tracking the action and outcome, learning through evaluations and adjusting or simply continuing is the process. It's not particularly difficult. It does require discipline that most people are not willing to invest. Most people choose not to be as deliberate as they could be and choose not to apply the discipline necessary to achieve continuous improvement in professional development.

It's all about choices, which is the very first step in decision making and a trustworthy gut.

9. Be accountable for your choices

It is easy to allow circumstances to be blamed for the outcomes you achieve. The truly growth oriented individual looks at the circumstances and determines their own role in creating those circumstances and owns their choices.

If you truly want to grow your business, every choice you make matters. Choosing to put up a large sign or a small sign, choosing to wait until the last minute to do something you have known about for weeks, putting off decisions the conditions for which will not change by waiting, choosing to do 20 things instead of 5, choosing to spend an entire day saving money by driving instead of flying, choosing to set the bar at achievable instead of remarkable, choosing to make commitments you have no idea how you will honor and then doing nothing to figure it out, these are all "the easy path".

When you choose to want to grow your business, you must also choose to be a new person. You must be willing to make choosing the best course a habit. Mark Zuckerberg eliminated one choice from his daily routine, his attire. Others have the same breakfast every day, the same lunch, go to the same restaurant, almost always, to allow themselves to be present for all the actual decisions/choices that need to be made over the course of their day.

Find out what you take for granted about your choices by holding yourself accountable for all your outcomes— the good and the bad. Be bigger than your business and hold yourself accountable. This is YOUR watch and what happens on YOUR watch is up to you. Choose thoughtfully. But, most importantly, always consciously choose.

10. Did you do all you could?

I hear "that doesn't work for my business" all the time. Sometimes, this message is driven by stories within an industry. Sometimes this is driven by a past experience 10 years ago. Sometimes it's something else. But, all the time, my role is to ask "how did you come to that conclusion." And the answers from that question get very fuzzy.

In order to know whether something worked or did not work, one needs to evaluate the effort put into making it successful. You can't simply make the claim you tried it and it didn't work. Just because you did it, does not mean you did it as well as it could have been done.

Take a trade show. I often hear that certain shows "work" and other shows "don't work" based on the one or two time experience of the exhibitor. When I query about what does a show effort look like, it boils down to put a bunch of stuff in a booth in an aisle of a show and talk to whomever walks into the booth.

A trade show is a temporary showroom in the downtown of an industry. Showing up with your stuff is the minimum that can be accomplished. Typically, that's why the results are minimal as well.

As you evaluate what you have done, be very clear that you are evaluating the How you did it aspect. If you did not do "all you could" then your conclusion is not sound.

More importantly, if you did not do "all you could", ask yourself why, and figure out how to do "all you can" next time. Better forethought creates clearer hindsight. Impulsive efforts can't provide any valuable hindsight at all. If you have no valuable hindsight, you can never really know how you are doing.

11. The physics of business

We tend to overlook the more simple aspects of business in general. Take something appearingly complicated that is actually relatively easy to understand like Newton's First Law of Motion. You've heard it if not actually studied it in high school. "An object in motion tends to stay in motion. An object at rest tends to stay at rest." This is how we remember the "law". We see it every day in hundreds of still items that need a push and lots of moving objects that continue unless stopped. But, there is a phrase as Newton penned his observation of the law that we forget that I did not include in the recollection above; "unless acted upon by an unbalanced force".

On an open field a soccer ball keeps rolling until friction from the grass and gravity make it stop. Then the ball stays stopped until it is kicked again. The unbalanced force is the kicking of the ball.

The unbalanced force in your business or your life is YOU and your collective company's efforts. Want sales to grow? You'll need an unbalanced force toward that outcome. That means you'll need to exert more energy/resources/creativity into the effort to get it moving forward than whatever you're doing now. By definition, whatever you're doing now is providing the exact amount of returns that is proportional to the current effort. Therefore, to make it change, you must infuse it with energy to propel it further.

Want to get more visitors to your website? You need to exert an unbalanced force of energy/resources/creativity toward that end.

Want to be better at something? You need to exert an unbalanced force of energy/resources/creativity to developing that improvement.

The balanced force creates equilibrium – no change at all.

The universe as well as the marketplace responds to unbalanced forces. Those forces, thoughtfully crafted, strategically deployed with disciplined execution, move objects from rest to motion or if already in motion change trajectories of products, brands or people's lives.

Where are you exerting unbalanced forces in your business or your life that will get you to where you want to go? Your alternative is to not exert any unbalanced forces in which case you are most likely to stay exactly where you are. That choice is yours.

12. New Year's Eve - Determine the year ahead

The amazing amount of enthusiasm for the new year and what it may hold is upon us. What does the New Year hold for us. Prosperity? Hardship? Opportunity? Challenge? Exciting new relationships?

We don't know, which is precisely why this moment is so important. Tomorrow the calendar will read 2015. Tomorrow, the slate of successes and failures in 2014 are erased, to be replaced over the year with new successes and failures.

I believe we put ourselves in the position to see opportunity. I believe those that lift their heads above the masses will see possibilities that others will not. Those people will be in positions where they cross paths with exactly what they need when they need it.

My preference is to determine where I want to go and head in that direction. In that case, I become determined. It is with this determination that opportunity will become more visible as I look only for the things that will get me closer to my destination and turn me away from the things that move me away from my destination.

Even so, if the amazing opportunity presents itself and looks to be perhaps a better suited destination, I am willing to change course, but, the opportunity will have to be significantly better than that which I am already pursuing.

In this way, I achieve focus. Focus on the destination. I am not oblivious to the rest, just determined to not miss that which I have set out to achieve in favor of some shiny object that may only be a distraction and cost me time in getting to the destination I wanted in the first place.

What is your destination this year? How are you getting there? What are you going to stop looking at in order to be able to focus on your destination? How determined are you? A flag in the wind has no determination. Don't be a flag in the wind. Determine your destination. Then chart a course and navigate it with determination. How will you know on this date next year, how well you did navigating your course?

Your Business Philosophy

13. Building a Smarter Business – The Business Model

Before actually getting to the Proof of Concept, one needs to explore and eventually choose the business model they intend to pursue. The two are intertwined, this article covers the business model.

In any consumer product, there are myriad ways to put products out to consumers. Your first awareness is do you have a "product" opportunity, or a business opportunity. They are very different and require very different resources over time.

You can be phenomenally successful with a single product. If you decide early on that you don't actually plan to build a company (lots of products over time), then you just sell as many of your product as possible in as little time as possible. It's a market assault all about your product. This focus approach to your business model will eliminate much of the investments in time or money you might consider. If your product is just a product, there is no need to build an entire infrastructure to support an entire range of related products.

You may elect to start with one business model and evolve into a different business model. Maybe you will sell on weekends at street fairs, sell to local retailers, sell online, sell at Amazon, sell at Walmart or national chains, etc. All of these choices can evolve or morph into a different kind of proposition. Generally speaking all the choices will be reduced down to two fundamentals – you are selling your products directly to consumers where you get the full retail value for the product, which is called direct to consumers, or you are selling your products to someone else who is using or selling the product to consumers, which is called wholesale.

Even within wholesale, plenty of companies make large successes out of selling to gift basket companies. You may have heard about all the "distributors" that sell to retailers. They are another path (mandatory in electronics). Then there is the custom imprint world from where you get your embroidered shirts and screen printed T-shirts. Your product may be more successful in Japan or France, an international distribution plan. Being clear on your path allows you to setup a financial model that can accommodate your gross margin needs to run the business.

Your end price, the price the consumer pays for your product, is completely determined by your business model and gross margin needs to run the business (provide you an income and pay for everything else). If you plan to sell directly to consumers at Amazon, you can sell at far lower pricing than if you are selling to a store. A store will "mark up" the product to sell it to consumers. The retailer needs to make money on the buying, stocking, staffing and selling of your products. Depending on the market channel or the retailer, that can be a small percentage of the final price or a very large percentage.

Setting your pricing by studying your market (it's not about being the low price leader, by the way), determining where your consumers will find your product interesting (consumers have habits and thought processes and don't buy bath towels at a plumbing store) and knowing what that particular effort will take to achieve in time and dollars, all by actually talking to people in the business, is exactly what is necessary to accomplish prior to making business model decisions to go forward.

14. Proof of Concept drives the investment

Many budding entrepreneurs are under the mistaken impression that coming up with a new idea, whatever it may be, has high value as though the idea is the value. As it turns out, having ideas for great products, and bringing products to life by proving they are sellable are two very distinctly different things.

The Proof of Concept, the actual products in the actual place where actual consumers or businesses buy the product, is exactly what makes an idea valuable. It's the proof. But, what constitutes a proof of concept can very often be misconstrued. Coming up with the most creative way ever to design a frying pan is not worth much. On the other hand, making the frying pan and putting it in front of people in a store, who then exchange cold, hard cash for the frying pan when compared to their other choices and then also knowing what it will take to scale the business, that, as we say in California, is gold.

By contrast, here's what are not proofs of concept. Creating a crowdfunding campaign and thinking that if 500 people are willing to invest $49 in the frying pan it will sell in stores at $49. Or, cooking your own salsa recipe and selling it at farmer's markets on weekends and thinking that this will be a slam dunk at grocery stores.

These are both valid proofs, if the goal is to sell frying pans via crowdsourcing or to sell salsa at farmer's markets. What I often hear is the product developer saying "this proves there is a market for my ...." In fact, both of these examples, the crowdsource and the weekend farmer's market, only prove that there is a market within the confines of the space selected. That is, crowdfunders are explorers and helpers, not competitive shoppers at kitchen stores. Weekend farmer's markets are people who are willing to buy fresh produce and artisanal items to start their weekends, not grocery store customers in a hurry to get in and out of the store.

When you're developing your Proof of Concept, be sure the Proof is of the actual Concept that you are planning to scale into the larger business. To prove a frying pan will sell in stores, it has to be in stores. To prove cheese will sell in stores, it has to be in stores. Failure to appreciate the concept that you're trying to prove may waste many months of your time and dollars from your pocket trying to take an inherently hobby business and turn it into a growth business. There is nothing wrong with a hobby business, but, just because something works in small scale has no bearing on whether it can be grown into large scale.

As an investor, I will immediately pay attention to the product that has already been in the market it wants to achieve (proven the concept). I also will immediately dismiss the product that has yet to find a place where success can be scaled (haven't finished their homework).

15. Effective communication is so rarely achieved

It is remarkable how many people think they are good communicators. Most people judge the effectiveness of their communication on what they say or write. But, there's a funny thing about communicating, if the other party doesn't get whatever it is you're trying to say – you fail. No grading, it's all pass/fail. It does not matter what you say, it is what is heard and understood that counts.

I saw a delightful exercise recently for a manager in training at a restaurant. In the restaurant parking lot, with the manager trainee's voice guidance alone, the trainee was to get her staff, one at a time and blindfolded, to walk through a little obstacle course in the parking lot. Each of the staff would have things in their hands and do some rudimentary tasks along the way, like set down or pick up a tray on a table.

It took the manager trainee numerous tries to realize you can't just say turn and go forward, you have to say turn left 90 degrees and take two steps forward. You can't say reach in front of you without saying how far or how fast because you might knock over exactly what was being reached for.

How many emails does it take you to provide explicit instructions about what you wish to have accomplished? How much ambiguity is there in everything you write? Ever read your emails as instruction sets?

If you're trying to be instructional, how are you layering your communication to be both encouraging and strict? If you're trying to be effective, how are you providing both the good with the bad?

Want to know how to tell? At your next meeting look at the your colleagues, the listeners for the results. If they are all nodding in agreement and walk away going in exactly the direction you expected, you were fantastic. If they go away and start asking "what did she mean", not good. If the creative person you just advised went away and then did something totally unexpected and off-course, you failed to communicate. Ever leave a meeting and wonder what it was about and who is going to do what by when? That's a fail.

Funny thing about communication, too. It is never the listener's responsibility to listen better (or read better). It is always the speaker's (or writer's) responsibility to convey the message better.

Great leaders are separated from good leaders by how well they communicate. Reread your emails. Reconsider your meetings or sales pitches. Revisit your website from a fresh vantage point. Is your message crystal clear so that anyone in your audience will easily get it? If not, change it!

Improve your communications and you will immediately see time savings. You will immediately see increases in productivity. Put the word CLARITY on a post-it note and attach it to the frame of your screen right now. Let it give you pause to increase your clarity.

And those of you who text a lot, you may very well be guilty of sloppy communication far more than you know, wasting hours and hours of you and your people's time when you think you are making it better. With communication happening via phone, email, text, post, Twitter, etc., becoming really, really effective at communication can propel you toward success faster than ever before.

16. A plan: something is always better than nothing

Start the Business with freshness – A Plan.

Plan: Noun

1. A scheme, program, or method worked out beforehand for the accomplishment of an objective

2. A proposed or tentative project or course of action

3. A systematic arrangement of elements or important parts; a configuration or outline

Plan: Verb

1. To formulate a scheme or program for the accomplishment, enactment, or attainment of

2. To have as a specific aim or purpose; intend

The Retirement Plan. The Vacation Plan. The Wedding Plan. The Renovation Plan. The Weekend Plans. The Family Reunion Plan. The Business Plan

All these plans simply describe in whatever detail what is to be done over a period of time to achieve an outcome. There are only two resources in your business; your time and your capital. And only one is renewable (it's the money). Do you have any idea how you are going to invest those two precious resources over the next 12 months?

This does not take weeks of thought. You're not writing for some competition (unless you are). You're simply doing what any worthwhile Financial Planner does. Look at your resources and work to determine where you can get "the biggest bang for your buck" and the greatest results from your time relative to achieving your desired goals. You do need to commit to the desire to maximize your options.

Here's a Start: Take ONE sheet of paper. Draw two vertical lines. Now draw three horizontal lines. You know have a grid of 3 columns and 4 rows. That's 12 months. January, February, March in the first row and so forth down the page.

In each box that is now a month, write in what you "plan" to do this month in terms of your efforts. Write in what you "plan" to spend of your capital in whatever areas. Those efforts will have outcomes you want to achieve. Write that in the appropriate month.

Trade show in March? Write it in. Needs $10,000 or you have $10,000 to invest? Write it in. You expect the show to generate $25,000 of sales (in March or in April or in each month after?). Write it in.

Get milestones into your plan; get the big account by; achieve sales volume of $xx by; introduce new products by. Get it on your calendar. Your schedule/calendar/plan is becoming real!!

If you make it more complicated you won't do it. Make it easier and you can do it **NOW**. Start every year with a Plan. Even a bad plan is better than no plan. "*If you fail to plan, you plan to fail*" Ben Franklin

Only 50% of wholesale businesses survive to year five. **Plan** to be a survivor.

17. Are you creating a job or a company?

When you create a new company by creating a product or products, you wear that all important hat of owner, the person in charge of growing the business and charting the course for the future. If you chose to create your company so that you would have a job that you control, that is not being the owner (by the definition above). You may be doing work that you find fulfilling, but someone still has to be the owner.

This is an ongoing dilemma for lots of startups. Somewhere in the early stages, the comfort zone gets stretched or the time that can be devoted to what the founder finds fulfilling gets squeezed. At that point, the owner has a set of interesting choices and decisions.

At this juncture, the owner has to determine which of the myriad responsibilities that are on the horizon are going to be something the owner wants to grow into being capable of owning, or would they prefer to delegate that to another. In its simplest form, this is the first step of scaling the business. Many owners have no idea what responsibilities are coming any more than a 4th grader knows what they will learn in 7th grade.

For a successful owner, willingness to dive in versus reluctance to engage is a defining awareness that those areas will soon come to a dead stop. The owner unwilling to take action or delegate responsibility is telling the marketplace and themselves "this is not our direction".

And of course, there is nothing wrong with that, as long as that is a decision and not avoidance. As a decision, that lays out the course for the company creating clarity of direction. As an avoidance it simply adds a backlog of "issues not addressed" which in my experience just becomes a longer and longer list.

For people new to being the owner (entrepreneurs), confronting the difficult may challenge the picture of their business that they had in their minds and can become completely paralyzing. Once created, momentum is very easy to lose and retrieval requires renewed and redoubled energy. Developing a strong sense of what an owner will be engaged in and what they will delegate is the very first step toward professional management of the business, be it by the owner or someone else. Putting decision making in the hands of people, experienced or hungry to learn and eager to take on new challenges is how companies thrive.

18. Are you well versed in your business? It rarely shows in the Sharktank.

If you watch Sharktank, you'll see presenter after presenter seeking financing for their business in one form or another. Each of them does some sort of product demonstration. Often times that presentation stops at the handing out of samples or passing around of the item amongst the sharks.

What I always find amazing is how many times the presenter, who is usually the company owner, needs to be asked about the "business" itself. It got me to wondering how many business owners are actually out of touch with any of their business metrics. We're not talking about Ford or General Electric here. These are small businesses that are closely held by the owners. So what could they be including? Let's try these.

Topline revenue – How much in sales of the product has been done in two recent periods? This shows the relative growth. This is a trailing indicator because it shows only history.

Total bookings – If there are orders outstanding that are not actually revenue yet, how much are they? Bookings is a leading indicator, which means it provides a window into the future revenues of the business.

Gross Margin on the above numbers, as a percentage or a number – That's the top margin number. Many businesses calculate this number differently. My personal preference is to take invoice totals, minus COG, minus freight, minus cost of warehousing and fulfillment, minus any discounts. The end result is how much money is left to spend on the rest of the business activity.

Store count (accounts or actual doors) – If you don't know this, there's trouble.

Inventory in dollars on hand – If you're selling a consumer product, your future sales are determined by inventory value on hand and gross margin. If gross margin is 50% and there is $40,000 in inventory, then that inventory can only create $80,000 in sales (40,000/50%). Which means once sold there will only be $40,000 to spend on sales, marketing, product development and running the business.

This information is not all on one report. Some are from the balance sheet. Others are from the P&L. Some software doesn't even keep track of bookings. No software calculates door count.

At the very simplest level, these 5 pieces of information would impress any prospective investor. Choose from these or find your own and know them, watch them and own them. I've always lived by bookings which requires timely processing of orders into an accounting package. These are what determines the financial health of your business.

19. 7 basic strategies your business needs to have

The strategy driven company can create plans. The plans will be developed with the strategy in mind. If the following 7 Strategies are not familiar in your company, big or small, make the time to work through them. Don't spend your time simply doing the work that is staring you in the face. Sustainability (in economic terms) comes far, far sooner to those that have a strategy for how to achieve it.

Sales Strategy – How are we going to create and maintain relationships with the buyers of the appropriate categories with the retailers we want to do business? How do we find them? How do we educate them? How do we treat them?

Trade Marketing Strategy – How are we going to become visible and relevant to new retail customer outlets? Do we send catalogs? Do we attend shows? Which ones? When and Why?

Consumer Demand Strategy – How are we going to ensure that we have a growing group of consumers who care about what we do/make? In store message? Social Media? PR? Website?

Distribution Strategy – How are we going to ensure that our products can be sold at all the locations that we want to attract? How will fulfillment be handled? How will products flow from wherever they are made (or even within the supply chain) to wherever the retailers are located?

Product Development Strategy – Where do we want to be in stores in next year, in 3 years or 5 years. What kinds of products might we need to get there? Which ones sooner? Which ones later?

People Strategy – What kinds of people do we need to have on the team (full time, part time, contracted, consulting) in order to be able to do all of the things above?

Finance Strategy – What kinds of financial capability do we need to have in place in order to become a $XXXX company, or to grow by triple (or tenfold or whatever it is for you) in the next XX months/years?

These 7 strategies are vital to the medium and long term success of the business. They should be vivid in your mind and documented somewhere for ongoing reference. They are your guide to all decision making. If you don't have plans that you are pursuing that integrate into these strategies, you are likely expending resources in areas unnecessarily. If you're too busy to do this, as a company owner, you have other challenges you need to address quickly. This is THE essence of making your business sustainable. Without this you are winging it – which is not sustainable.

20. Are you working for results or for a wage?

In this past year, we have twice made offers for purchasing consumer product businesses. In both cases, I was surprised by the perspective that each owner had about how much their business was worth, based on the amount of time they had invested in it. It seemed so irrelevant to me.

Each of these opportunities came about because the owner was winding down in their physical capacity to keep up the pace. Both were 100% DIY propositions. That means the owner did all the sales, all the fulfillment or delivery, all the marketing, all the inventory planning, all the order taking, etc. One even made the product himself.

Both businesses had also provided some form of income for the owners over many years. Both businesses provided one low wage job; a job that required someone to wear a dozen hats, but, still only one job.

When we evaluated the businesses and looked at what had been accomplished from the outside, it was not very much. The businesses had ebbed and flowed with the capacity of the owner. When the owner took an extended vacation, the business suffered. When the owner did a trade show, the business had a mild upswing. When the owner failed to do enough follow-up, the business sank back.

The results these businesses had created over some many, many years, were not encouraging. Sales were declining as a result of the owners realization that they had reached their limit on DIY. The bottom line (profits) was non-existent, partly because the business had been run more like a personal checking account and partly because the overall income was so low.

When we made our offer based on results, both sellers found our offer grossly low because it did not come close to paying for "all the time" they had put into their business.

A business is not valued by how much time someone has put into creating it. Accomplishment is the best internal and external measure of both. In both cases, the owner was able to create a living for themselves all those years, a job being self-employed. How much would anyone "pay" to buy a job?

As a business owner, I get the expectation of paying for results. Having been a wage earner, where I do what is asked of me, I get that understanding, too. As we all work to grow our businesses, we need to be very conscious of how many ways we can create the appropriate results and expectations for all involved so as not to be simply doing work on a daily basis because it's there. I can move a pile of dirt from one place to another indefinitely and get paid a wage. As a business owner, I need to be laser focused on ensuring that moving the pile of dirt is the most valuable thing needs to be done and that I am the person to do it. Otherwise, I should be finding someone else to move the pile while I do what I can to grow the business.

Just because work exists in a business does not mean it needs to be done by you. Staying focused on the highest priorities is critical to increasing the value of your business, and your life.

21. Contractor's syndrome; how something you're capable of doing just never gets done

Have you heard about how the contractor's house is never finished? I always thought it was because the contractor didn't really want to do the work in his spare time that he does for a living. This week I found an alternate point of view that made sense for far more than just the contractor.

The contractor is totally CAPABLE of doing the work to finish his house himself (DIY). Why would he hire someone to do the work? He wouldn't. Each of the unfinished projects will take 3 hours, but, week after week goes by and somehow the contractor never finds the 3 hours. Weeks lead to months. This is the "contractor's syndrome".

The time it takes to do something is often confused with how quickly it will be completed on a calendar. There are two measurements of time – the time to perform the work, and the time on the calendar by which the work will be complete. Both are necessary to be aware of and use in considering whether to DIY or to hire someone to do it.

We all have examples in our work of the small project that is not getting finished. Maybe it is not fun. Maybe you are not good at it (but you know how). Maybe you need one tool or one piece of information. Whatever the case is, you are not getting to it. You know it will only really take 3 hours (or less), yet, there it sits month after a month. Why? Because it never rose high enough on your priority list to become important to complete, which absolutely does NOT mean it is not important to the organization. Remember, the contractor (and his family) are living in the unfinished house.

Soon enough, these projects multiply (at the contractor's house) and one becomes 3, becomes 5, becomes 10. Now there is real time required. And in your business, you are still fully capable of doing them yourself, you just don't get to them as other higher priorities continue to arise.

When you let your capabilities define your priorities and your work load, you are losing ground every day. Your company needs you to define your company priorities and develop your capabilities accordingly. Then your company needs you to outsource or hire the rest.

For the contractor, the priority is the client's house, not his own house. He should hire the people to finish his house. For your company, the priority is and you need to find other people to take care of the rest. The longer you wait, the more that piles up, and the more calendar you lose (which can't be reclaimed). Start setting priorities and stop giving up calendar. Make your company capable of more than just what you can do yourself.

22. You can't do it all

Many business startups (founders) wonder over time why their business has yet to achieve the level of success that their early efforts made seem so inevitable. Having been in that position myself, I came to learn a significant lesson and now can share the awareness with you.

All new businesses are built on the hopes and dreams of the startup team or person. That typically means the founder(s) has conceived of and developed some product or service that resonates for a given group (the niche). Once conceived and developed, the founder contacts the first targets for converting the product or service to commerciality and succeeds in gaining some revenue from some of them. What happens next becomes the complicated structure that determines the future success of the business.

When the entrepreneur is confronted with success, these successes usually create additional support work of some type. An infrastructure becomes necessary to take care of the ongoing efforts to invoice, collect payments from the Customer and deposit it in the bank. In a consumer product business, this single action is complicated by the need to acquire the item to be sold, take an order from a customer, move the item from wherever it is to where the customer wants it and then do the steps above. Anyone can foresee the steps, however few can foresee the challenges when the scale begins to escalate. I never did.

When the first customer comes to the business (even on the internet), the founder supports that customer. When the customer makes suggestions, the founder listens. Almost from the outset, the founder is confronted with additional workload that is not increasing sales. This effort is operations. And because it is a necessary part of getting paid for the product or service, every founder needs to have a plan for how to implement, manage and make it scalable.

Interestingly, most don't. Instead, they DIY or hire some person to wear a lot of hats, hoping that they will be self-managing. Eventually, that person hires someone else and the story plays out with hire after hire, distraction after distraction. As sales increase, so do the number of needs the business has and therefore the number of people needed to fill those needs.

After all the thoughtful effort put into the development of the product or services, to get it just right, and then have actual customers willing to pay actual money, it's so tempting to simply hire the most capable person you can find who is coincidentally available at that time. And therein the cycle begins. I know, we did it unknowingly for quite a few years.

I don't know how much sales we lost while working to accommodate all our growth internally. I know we had extended plateaus in sales during periods of operational expansion. Grow. Plateau. Grow. Plateau. We vividly saw the plateau, but, had no idea why. We thought it was the marketplace until many years later and we realized each sales growth spurt was followed by a plateau as we built infrastructure. Accommodating yesterday or today, we pulled our focus away from the growth efforts for tomorrow – Product Development, Marketing and Sales – that would fuel the longer term.

Each time we had to work to expand our operations infrastructure to accommodate a major customer, or a high performing sales person, or a successful trade show, we weren't working on the new products, the marketing or the ongoing sales. There are only so many hours in a day or a week. The calendar waits for no one.

23. Decide to Decide

It's very easy to allow a decision to linger. You know all the reasons, more info, more data, more communication, more insight, more, more, more. Many decisions we leave open in hopes they will simply evaporate all by themselves, which is sort of a decision itself.

There is an interesting linguistic core to this "indecision-ness". The core word of decide, cide or "cida", which is latin for kill. Homicide is to kill a human. Suicide is to kill yourself, etc. Decide is to kill all the other options that are in front of you and accept the one remaining.

Think about the last decision you made, maybe for breakfast. What one thing did you choose and therefore kill off all the other choices that you could have had for breakfast?

I would go a bit further in the business sense. Every decision not made today, kills the calendar another day. It leaves that decision, big or small, hanging around to do additional damage through added weight of existence. 500 or 1000? This layout or that layout? These colors or those colors? Call back today or tomorrow? Whatever the decision is, if you're not waiting for a specific piece of already identified further information and know when you will have it, MAKE THE DECISION now. You can generally recover from poor decisions. Likely the margin of "bad-ness" in your decision is marginal anyway. The only way to get better at making decisions is to...............make LOTS of decisions.

In my years as a sports referee (basketball, soccer, baseball and volleyball), the amount of time allowed to make a decision was in the moment. Those years of virtually spontaneous decision making proved invaluable for me in now being able to make all kinds of decisions thoughtfully and quickly. Read the rule book (be prepared with the info you need), then make the decision and move on. It's not hard. But, the game that is your business can't go on if the decisions aren't made. Imagine the fan uproar at the sports event when the whistle blows and the referee signals that he wants to "think about it".

Where is your business not going forward because you aren't making a decision? Then decide to start deciding!!

24. Your process vs. Getting results

The more you have personally taken on to get where you are, the more likely you are to think that the process you used to get there is THE best process out there.

If you created your product descriptions, or you created your "streamlined" movement of information, or you have created your supply chain top to bottom, you will be very likely to want to have it done that way because "that's the way we do it (that's the way I did it)".

However, and there is always a however, what if that way you did it met the needs of the past and will not the needs of today or the future? What if that way is actually more cumbersome, only you did not recognize it because you were just looking for a solution that would work and didn't know what others know or just never considered other options?

The very first lesson in owning your own business is the sooner you can become results focused and stop being process focused, the sooner you can achieve the results that you so desperately want to create.

Sure, there are sacred processes. There always are. Protect those with all your energy. If your business has a "way you do it" because it is vital to your story or message, vital to your quality, vital to your community, and that is what your Customers are paying for, then by all means maintain those. But, when the process is "this was the best idea I had at the time and I'm pretty proud to have created it", that standard is too low. Let others create their own processes in order to get you even better results than you had before.

You can only grow past your own efforts by entrusting others, showing them where you want them to be and giving them the time and resources to get there. That is leadership. Leadership gets the most out of others. Supervising tells other people what to do and how to do it. Leader or Supervisor? You choose.

25. Deserve vs. Earn

The word deserve is gets a lot of mileage even becoming part of a few of Scott Adams' Dilbert cartoons. As a business owner or commission based worker for almost my entire career, I find deserve an interesting term and am wondering what happened to "earned".

Without question there are things we as humans deserve and the list has possibilities for being long or short depending on who you are and your own personal perspective. Where I have become curious is whether or not the word deserve is beginning to impose on earn and started to make the two words interchangeable. Examples? Sure.

Someone works really hard over a weekend and gets time off; do they deserve it or did they earn it? Someone gets a raise because their work is exemplary; do they deserve it or did they earn it?

When someone does not get time off (their coworker does) because they did not work really hard over a weekend do *they* deserve time off? They certainly did not earn it.

This is my confusion. I've always believed that in order to get what one personally feels they "deserve" they have to earn it. I think successful business people also feel that way. Just because someone wants it, or just because others have it, does not equate to whether or not someone has made the investment of themselves to earn it.

Business people can sometimes get caught in the trap of comparing their effort, their product, their investment of themselves in some comparative way to others and because someone else got a particular outcome from their effort or investment, that they too in fact deserve that outcome. That's a really dangerous perspective to have in a competitive landscape.

In every competitive situation, which is where we all are every day, there are winners and there are losers. In a sporting sense between two competitors, they may both put out the same amount of energy and compete for the same amount of time, maybe even have practiced the same amount, but, for some reason, one wins and the other loses. Who deserved it and who earned it?

Vocabulary is a powerful tool. Great business leaders use words very carefully. To earn people's respect, be thoughtful with yours.

26. Having goals is a start – Actions to achieve goals makes them real

I talk to lots of entrepreneurs who have wonderfully prepared or identified the goals they want to achieve for the year. I find far fewer entrepreneurs that actually have a plan of actions they are taking to achieve those goals.

It is easy to understand that in order to achieve a goal of running a marathon that one must consistently run increasingly longer distances to get in shape to run the marathon. The action to achieve the goal is to block out increasing amounts of time to run increasingly longer distances. No time commitment. No running. No marathon goal achieved. The goal will be achieved by running (action) but, without the time commitment the running can't happen. The time commitment predicament is exactly why over 80% of gym memberships go unused after 4 weeks.

Entrepreneurs get caught in this goals/actions trap all the time (everyone does for that matter). Stuff comes up. Opportunities. Events. Old habits. All kinds of stuff. Now is exactly the right time to look at your calendar and assess how your time commitment (and therefore your actions) is propelling you to achieve your goals. If it's not on your calendar, it's likely not going to happen. Block it out. Block it out like you might block out a workout at the gym on Tuesday and Thursday at 7am. Your calendar (if you respect it) will then MAKE the time for you to achieve your goals. Achieving your goals, like a lot of things, starts with showing up. Your calendar can tell you to show up.

27. Every day is new information

As business owners, we gather information every day from lots of places. We read the news. We talk to vendors. We talk to sales people. We talk to customers. We attend trade events. There is no shortage of ways to be informed about the market in which your product exists.

The most important thing you can do with those conversations is to listen and evaluate what you are hearing and continually ask yourself whether the perspective you are observing is supporting the success of your company strategy or eroding the success of your company strategy.

Each day you have 24 new hours by which to evaluate your Company direction and success in making progress toward your business goals. Each day, the information you acquire from your conversations and observations can provide you with valuable gems of knowledge that may cause you to think twice, reevaluate, reconsider, confirm, affirm or obliterate the ideas or plans you had the day prior.

You need to be listening for them. You need to be thinking that way, every day. Running your growth business is not a job, it's a responsibility. Your vendors, your Customers, your consumers, they represent your organization and they are counting on you to do all you can to be more viable tomorrow than you are today. To be more healthy and more thoughtful.

Every day, you have the opportunity to leave everything in your business just as it was yesterday, or to change it. For some that is too much to fathom and they pay no attention to what they observe except once a year. Each day they continue to do what they did the day before. For others, they tweak their strategy all the time not really secure in the fundamentals of where they are going or the viability of their strategy.

Your strategy is your holy grail. Own it and find those that will support it with you, economically. Find tactics that you can use or abandon all the time. Be a great listener and observer and an even better implementer. Evaluate what is possible in what time frames at what cost and what value and what is the mountain of work that may need to be entered into judiciously. The dividends to be gained from deeply paying attention to what you are seeing, hearing and observing are priceless.

28. What is the Good Enough standard for your business

Every business would love to answer phones on the first ring, respond to emails in 5 minutes, ship orders the same day, have zero defects or errors and achieve perfection at everything they do. The reality is, very, very few businesses have the resources to achieve that lofty standard.

Most companies then make "compromises" along the way. Generally, there are a few things that they do really well, and a bunch of stuff that is OK or even kind of poor. They expend lots of energy on really being terrific at something, maybe the product, or the order turnaround or something, but tend to not even look at the rest of the business.

Interestingly, when the thing that is terrific is so incongruent with the other areas of the business, or if one other thing is disproportionately poor compared to the rest, the customer will no longer see what the company is terrific at and only focus on the bad stuff.

It's no secret that a reputation can be crushed online. What can take months, even years to develop through consistent performance can be ruined by one bad situation. Have you ever noticed how much a company suffers online because one situation was not addressed thoughtfully? And it's never about responding in 5 minutes, it's about being thoughtful.

There is a saying I learned from T. Harv Eker a long time ago; "How you do anything is how you do everything."

Set a standard of "acceptable" (good enough) and then do it **EVERYWHERE ALL THE TIME**.

Figure out where your company can afford to be with money or time, where it needs to be competitively and then meet that standard in everything you do. Have you ever gone into an awful bathroom at a restaurant and immediately wondered if the kitchen was clean?

It is far, far more valuable to be consistent at everything than to be incredible at a couple of things and miserable at others. Sustainability for your business is measured by the systems and practices you embed in the business, not the one star thing you might be most proud of. Your reputation depends on your consistency. Consistency is where your business teaches your customer how to set their expectation in the first place!

Whatever "good enough" is for your company, do it everywhere. You set customer expectations through your entire business, not just the few things you do well.

29. Water Runs Downhill

We all know that water runs downhill. We learned it maybe even before we were in school. We also know that water on earth is at the heart of life.

Now look at your business and where you are working really hard and making little progress and ask yourself how many different ways are you trying to make water go uphill. What process, project or issue are you struggling with right now, that if only you removed the dam or changed the waterway, would flow like the Amazon River.

Now, imagine extending that effort into relieving not just the obstacle directly in front of you, but, the ones further down that waterway channel as well. That process is at the core of forethought. As the executive of your business, it desperately needs you to be able to look down river, anticipate impediments and find or create the right waterway channels for your business to become broad and deep.

As you confront the daily challenges of working at your business, put as much time as possible into looking at every situation and extending it down the channel a few miles and see what outcomes you can envision. Make darn sure you love those outcomes, because once you send the first drops of water down the waterway, they go exactly where water goes, downstream.

To really progress, make notes in some way about what you expect. Looking back at those notes regularly will tell you everything about how you are doing in ways that a P&L or a Balance sheet cannot. In your business, you are Lewis and Clark with far, far more tools than they had crossing the U.S. on rivers 200 years ago. Yet, they took copious notes we still refer to today about conditions then. The future of your business depends on you being equally diligent.

30. Will Santa fill your wish list?

We're always so hopeful at the beginning of every year now 12 months. Four weeks ago we celebrated Thanksgiving at which time many, but, not all, would have been grateful for the wonderful year they had and how well their business fared over the course of the year.

Now we find ourselves at Christmas where many of us are hopefully reviewing the shortcomings of the previous year by virtue of the observation that we now have a wish list of things that we planned or hoped for but did not materialize. Maybe your wish was 10x growth or 50% growth or adding 5 new major accounts or maybe one.

If you found yourself with a list of unfulfilled wishes for the past year, now is exactly the time to look deeply into your own efforts and figure out how not to repeat them. If you subscribe to the perspective as I do, that our position is the direct reflection of the sum of the effort we put into getting there, then this can be a highly introspective, self-evaluating moment.

But, if you don't want to do the hard work of looking at yourself and how your situation is exactly what you have created, there is always next year, to simply do it again which will very likely achieve precisely the same results. The choice is always yours.

31. Price, Service, Quality – Make price last not first

This is an old concept that bears a revisit. Fundamentally, these are the three attributes that constitute value in any transaction: price, service and quality. When you want a dress or a pair of shoes, there are numerous places, designs, prices and qualities that are inherent in the overall buying experience and eventual satisfaction with the dress or shoes and your satisfaction with the outcome. Value is after all an assessment of the "worth" that something holds for the buyer.

The internet has disrupted our sense of "worth" and therefore value by placing an increasing focus on price as the distinguishing variable. Why pay 90 when you can get the same thing elsewhere for 88 is a fair question? But, to determine value over time, I want to be able to look at quality and service first and price last.

When you stay at certain hotels, the experience is much different than at other hotels. Addressing a problem you may encounter during your stay is much different. Even the sleep you get may be much different. Simply speaking, the quality of the experience and the services that can be provided can be vastly different.

The same is true of clothing. The experience you have with a garment or shoes over time – washing, fading, stitching, etc. can be very different from one garment or shoes to another. Therefore, knowing what you are seeking in the quality and service variables FIRST will guide you to price levels for the wearing/washing/lasting/looking experience you will have with the garment.

The internet makes it all too easy to sort by price and push decisions to be price based. I see purveyors of upmarket products continually shopping online for the "lowest price" and then being frustrated that some aspect of the "experience" goes badly.

If you are simply buying (or selling) commodities, by all means, get the best price for that commodity. If you are buying (or selling) things that will have "value" then make price the last consideration. Nothing makes tomorrow any more difficult than having a bad night's sleep, so don't blame the low priced hotel located next to a nightclub for your bad night's sleep. If you want to sleep well, figure out what that is worth to you (value) and then always be comfortable paying for it. When you don't get the value at the price, that's a different story.

32. You can't grow managing by individual data points

Consistently with small businesses I hear a similar line of reasoning that involves Customers, wants or direction. The thinking goes down one of these two paths. My existing Customers tell me….. or…. I sold a lot of these over a certain period of time.

The question is then "do you make decisions or choose direction based on an incredibly small amount of data points"; in fact, sometimes only one.

If you have sold 60 pieces out of 75 all to one Customer of the 8 that bought the product, can you make an observation that this is a good selling item or not? Can you make an observation about whether this product is productive for your entire company? For all your Customers? Can you even say whether there is any reason to keep it going forward?

No, you flat out can not because you need context about the one customer that bought 60. How did they get great results? Did they even get great results or did they give away 50 pieces in a promotion? Is this customer repeatable in the market place? Can you get 100 customers to get the same result?

There are dozens, hundreds and thousands of ways that single data points can kill your business, consume resources and waste calendar time, because you made black and white decisions based on some assumption you made about the very limited results you have seen thus far. Those decisions could encourage you to keep going or suggest you stop on a marketing effort, a product direction or even an entire strategy.

Don't get caught in a limited data decision without knowing everything about the limited data you have and match it to what you are working to achieve. When the knowledge of the limited data result is thorough, or the time has been allowed for limited data to become broad data, then make your decisions. In the meantime, keep going on the strategy, plan, effort you have laid out and get the data that you need.

When you look in and find that only 8 of 100 stores bought the product at all, it does not matter whether you have sold 60 to one or 75 to three or not. The problem is in the selling the product into the market.

If you can't get this level of understanding with the systems you have in place, you are the equivalent of driving a car at night with a flashlight and no gauges in the fog. Sure you might get where you are going or you might not and either way, it's going to be really slow, or really dangerous. Choice is yours.

33. Ambiguity vs. Precision

When do you need to be precise and when can you be ambiguous? That question comes up often and can be a defining issue when two parties involved in an activity together fail to communicate the need for one or the other.

One of the primary breakdowns in relationships stems from the above conflict and the use of email and not phone calls to align the needs of both parties.

Ambiguity is fantastic for far off time frames, for opening dialogues and the like. Do speak in "ballpark" terms and possibilities when the dialogue is still in concept.

When the dialogue becomes more advanced, actual delivery dates, prices for specific quantities, payment timeframes, you must be accurate and precise.

Not sure? Find out by asking. Always take the time to learn and understand "terms of engagement" in any relationship, just as you might with a new friend. Find out how they operate. Find out what motivates them. Find out what makes them tick. Do all of this while it is still acceptable to be ambiguous. Once you become precise, you will need to deliver on what is now a promise.

Tell someone that the price is $1.03 and when they call to place a Purchase Order two weeks later for 10,000 pieces tell them you've had a price increase to $1.15 and see what happens. If you had only said the price will be less than $1.25, you could have quoted the price when they were ready to buy at the $1.15 and they would have been quite satisfied.

If you're not studying human behavior and learning about your customer's need for precision vs. ambiguity, you will be missing a significant part of the dynamics of relationships, be they seller-buyer, employer-employee, peer to peer or any other. Being precise when ambiguity will suffice and being ambiguous when precision is necessary can erode trust and confidence, two relationship components that can be difficult or expensive to repair once damaged.

34. Calendar equals commitment

I recently wrote a piece on Precision vs. Ambiguity. I thought I would take a minute to enhance that "conversational" perception and contrast it with a calendar reality.

Your calendar is the most vivid depiction of the priorities you have. Look at your calendar, sure, right now. If that's only in your mind, that's already a bad sign.

Is your calendar full of milestones and deadlines for things that are important in your world? Is it comprehensive? Can you tell someone when you want something completed by in order to have it available for whatever happens next?

Many people are good at planning for Holiday Shopping, a special party or a wedding and plan months in advance. Yet they may be terrible at planning out what needs to happen for their business in order to make it hum. Example: Put off finding the cake decorator or reserve the location you want for a wedding and you will get whatever is left uncommitted because the calendar eliminated choices as the event became closer. That's how it works. If it's important, do it sooner. To do that, put it in your calendar.

Milestones and deadlines should all be there – along with whatever interim things need to be called out so as not to be missed. When someone asks about the launch date, or the available date and you are ambiguous, it's because you are not driving your organization to get it done. To see if your company has direction, look deeply into your calendar. What does your calendar say about your ability "to get it done"?

Here is what I know. You can largely size up a person's or a company's priorities by their calendar. People who have lots of stuff on their calendars achieve things. People who keep it in their head or in disparate places they don't see every day don't achieve as many things. Why bury what's important in your world exclusively in the vault that is your overtaxed brain? What's on the calendar gets done. Simple. The bigger the impact you want to have with your efforts, the more people you need to rally to get stuff done, the more central your calendar is.

Next time you consider attending a Sports event or performance of some kind, any kind, ask yourself when that event was calendared by the participants? Run your business like everything you do is that important. Or ask yourself why not.

Your Path to Sales

35. B2C does not equal B2 (B+B+B+B) C

A prevalent myth about graduating from the B2C or from a crowd-funding campaign is to think that the wholesale effort of putting products into stores is simply "more of the same". Listening to Michael Houlihan, who with Bonnie Harvey created Barefoot Cellars wine, he articulated the challenge as he observed it through his development of the brand.

Mr. Houlihan got into the "wine" business and was certain that if he made a good wine, everything else would take care of itself because consumers would like his products. Therefore, he began to shape an awareness that selling to the consumer was the top priority.

As Barefoot started to expand past the enthusiasm of the people who drank the wine and liked it enough to give it an award or two, what Mr. Houlihan came to learn was that there were quite a few layers of selling that needed to go on and without selling to each layer, his brand would evaporate quickly no matter how many awards his brand earned.

What Mr. Houlihan articulated so wonderfully was the need to "sell" his own people on his vision of the business and the future, so they would all go out in the same direction. Then, he needed to sell the management of the Distributor on carrying the brand (and why). Then, he needed to sell the distributor sales manager and the sales people on selling the brand (and how). Then, he needed to sell the management of a retailer on carrying the brand in the store (and why). Then, he needed to sell the sales people in the store on selling the brand once it was in the store (and how).

Each of these participants in getting the product to the consumer had a different reason to move forward. The distributor carries a product for strategic reasons. The distributor sales people sell it for personal reasons (making money). The retailers buy it for the fit into the other products being carried and for the strength of the merchandising support that comes with the brand. The store staff sells the product because it creates happy consumers.

In a B2C world, assuming you make a quality product all the time, meeting the simple product delivery expectation of the end user/consumer is all that it takes to make happy customers. Once in the wholesale channel, there a number of other places that the brand must succeed in convincing others that the promulgation of the brand is in their interest.

Once Mr. Houlihan realized this sequence, they reassessed their entire business model and stopped seeking asset acquisition in production equipment or real estate, etc., and came to focus on the fact that their real business was "distribution management" which by his definition was all about sales at these different levels.

The sales effort is the doorway to success. Skip any levels of the process in sales and it is like trying to skip a few levels in a video game. You can't. You have to earn it. Make the calls. Mold the presentation into what is in it for the person on the other side. Don't skip the sales people of the distributor or retailer. Then figure out how to do it to the scale that you want to achieve.

Every store has plenty of inventory right now and does not truly need your new product at all. But, if you can make your compelling presentation to all the parties along the way as to why it should be your product, you'll get some space. When everyone can make money selling your product, that's what wins the day.

36. Why Sales People Matter: The 5 Roles of a Sales Person

A lot of businesses think that they can grow their business without "sales people". In all fairness, by some people's definition, they don't need sales people, because they find sales people "slimy" or superfluous. However, what I've come to discover through the years is that all businesses need sales people, it's just that many people are not willing to call them sales people.

It is particularly vivid in consumer products where there is a person for every retail store in the world who has a responsibility called "buyer". Everyone that buyer talks to that is not inside their organization is likely titled "seller". Where sellers and buyers meet is called a marketplace which is what creates commerce. That said, here are the roles a seller in the wholesale business must play, whether the people in the roles are called sales people or not.

Identify and make contact with buyers. Yes, this seems obvious, but, when you stand at a trade show for 3 days and you see nothing but buyers, it's easy to forget that the marketing vehicle called the trade show actually worked aggregating buyers with some of them coming to your booth and needing to speak to a "sales person".

Presenting products in a frame in which the buyer needs to hear it. You'd be shocked at how many unsuccessful sales people are only good presenters.

Presentation is important, but, only if it actually creates a spark in the buyer to want to move forward, which always boils down to "what's in it for me" and telling that story in a way that is meaningful to the buyer.

Progress the relationship. From the superficial initial contact to creating a working relationship between two companies is not like shopping at Amazon and clicking a product. It takes a lot of back and forth so the two companies can become engaged.

Closing. We've certainly seen some of the less impressive tactics used to sell a car. At its best, the process is about gaining mutual commitments, proving follow through and mutually impressing each other with discipline and diligence.

Ongoing Relationship Management. Every relationship needs to be nurtured and tended over time. Problems arise. Opportunities come forward. Challenges appear. All of this needs to be addressed in a timely manner to foster the long term health of the business together.

Whether you play these roles yourself, as a solo-preneur, put these roles on different people at different times, hire inside or outside people to do it, all of these efforts MUST be addressed to continually bring new opportunity to your business. Not every person in sales is good at all 5 roles. Most are not (most solo-preneurs are not either) which is why teams and support are there to enhance the parts that need it. Any business that overlooks any of these roles is simply breaking the definition of the marketplace – where sellers and buyers meet. Being good at selling is knowing which role you're playing at any given time. Skip or ignore any of the roles at your own peril.

37. Your products are only as good as the sales team

Do you have a sales team that is excited about your newest products? Are they hungry to go out and sell these items into your Customer's stores? How long will it take for your new product to be seen by all your existing Customers?

Most small companies have no answers to these questions. Many companies that rely exclusively on Distributors don't even know who the sales people are, whether they are excited or how long it takes to be seen by existing Customers.

Other companies have lots of sales people and don't give them the tools they need prior to the availability of the product so that those sales people can succeed out of the blocks.

Other companies still are under the impression that sales people are an extraneous expense and therefore don't have any at all.

If any of these are your Company, you are doing your growth rate and your future a huge disservice by not investing smartly in a sales network.

The outside investor or any general manager looking at your company from the outside will judge it's overall value by three things – it's sales capability, it's distribution capability and it's Customer base. Those three elements are the pipelines to growth. Those three elements ensure a long term ability to put new products into the marketplace. Lack of those three elements is a giant constraint to growth and makes your Company a target for competitors not to mention makes growth incremental not exponential.

One huge reason entrenched players win more often is because they have these three networks dialed in and productive.

Want to reach your dreams for your products and your company? Focus on building financially lucrative relationships with sales people. You can never have too much sales!!!

38. 7 tips to make buying from you and your sales people easier

When you go to a new restaurant do you ever ask the waitress what she recommends or what the best sellers are? And when you do, does she have an answer?

A lot of brands are unprepared to communicate simplicity to retailers. Why, because it's easier to simply produce a catalog.

The smart restaurateurs train their wait staff to know what the best sellers are and what the recommended offer should be, because this is what is the very most likely to make the guest happy with their experience. Those dishes are not necessarily better than the others, they are just far more likely to create loyalty by the customer because they will provide a proven positive experience.

Loyalty from a retailer comes from sell through. Simple as that. An empty shelf gets refilled. Looking at your business make sure your sales materials and sales people have these elements (tools) at their disposal all the time:

1. All items in your catalog and online have item numbers listed (not UPC numbers, they are too long).

2. Items that are newer are called out from the ones that are older assisting existing customers to find what they may wish to refresh the merchandise statement.

3. Organize your catalog and price list so that it is easy to cross reference.

4. Give your sales people a list of the top sellers in each of the categories in which you classify your products. (Do you know your best sellers in each category?)

5. Give your sales people 3 opening order assortments. One at lower investment, one at medium investment and one at high investment, depending on your price points.

6. Give your sales people photos or samples of the instore signage or other store photos that will allow the retailer to visualize the presentation in their store that will create the "sell through" needed to succeed.

7. Provide an order form – even if no one uses it. It's a guide and a Call to Action. Be sure it contains any specific terms of doing business with your company.

Next time you're in a successful restaurant that attracts new customers all the time, look at their communication systems and think of your sales process. What else can you do to make it easier and easier to buy your products?

The winner of shelf space is generally not the coolest product, it is the one with the best communication tools for the salespeople to remain engaged with the retailers and consumers. The higher level of trust goes to the brands that communicate well. Always be making the sales process easier or you surely you will be making the sales process harder.

39. Founder as Presenter-OK: Founder as Salesperson-RISKY

Everyone wants to be able to stand and deliver a product presentation like Steve Jobs. Turns out that's not hard, if the audience is a room full of avid followers, the advance hype has been high and the name on your product is Apple. It may even be recommended. I'm talking here about confusing presenting with selling.

No one, particularly a retail buyer, wants to hear a long drawn out story of the toils your company went through to get to today, the hard work of the company to produce what it makes, the 1001 reasons the product is great. What the retail buyer wants to know is how much is it and what will my customers know about this product before they see it. What will drive them to see it?

The store buyer is in the business of make money selling the products they select to put in their store, which is now almost always an unassisted sales environment. Therefore, what story does your packaging tell about your product? How is your company going to support the retailer for sell through (marketing, advertising, social media, etc.)?

If you are a new supplier to that retailer, there is every chance the retailer is already concerned that you don't actually realize what it will take to support the sales in the store, with additional inventory, with in-store signage, whatever. "Yes, thank you for creating this amazing product, but, no one is going to see it to buy it, so tell me about your investment in sales and consumer facing marketing."

Steve Jobs always had the history of Apple and the passionate Apple consumers, not to mention stores that had an Apple sign over the doorway and a heavily assisted sales environment. As the newest vendor in the store, you will have exactly zero of that. So how do you go from being nobody to getting into the store? You sell!

By selling you ask questions. You want to learn how to serve this Customer, the retailer (not the consumer) to make money in the space. What is needed for the retailer to succeed? Remember they are looking for ROI, not amazing new product. Learning how to be a partner through questions is not presenting. What we saw of Steve Jobs was not selling – it was presenting.

Want to know why the incumbent's version of a product gets placement and the new guy does not? The retailer has every reason to trust the incumbent since they are already making money together. Would you hire a new financial planner if your current financial planner is already delivering results that satisfied your expectation? Of course not. Then why expect the retailer to do it by throwing out a vendor in favor of you and your product.

Selling is part of a dialogue. Presenting is a monologue. Founders talk 80% about themselves. Sales people talk 80% about the buyer. You want to win shelf space? Start by meeting the needs of the retailer (your Customer) and not just making a good product with a great product presentation.

40. Identify the opportunity first with everyone

Most people think that in order for a buyer at a retail store to buy a product, they have to "like" or "understand" the product somehow. As a result, many presenters focus their conversations all the time, regardless of the listener, on the product itself. Sharktank has many great examples of inventors who have yet to really understand fully what the full circle of selling consumer products is all about.

A good buyer is looking for products she can sell, not use personally. That means products that her Customers will want to buy. It's about the money after all. A buyer tries to figure this out when looking at a new product by thinking about the other products in the category, what is working, what is not and whether this product, by virtue of its package, uniqueness or story will be able to outsell or enhance sales of the department.

The smart seller does homework to understand the buyer's department and uses that awareness in crafting a fit for her product in the buyer's product mix. This is the "opportunity" section of the conversation which is always first. What opportunity, for the retailer, does your product meet. If there is no meeting of the minds on the opportunity, the product is irrelevant for the buyer (don't bother with the demo!).

When the buyer agrees with the opportunity, the door opens to your product and how your product is uniquely positioned to meet that opportunity for the buyer.

Having been a road sales guy, I can truly attest to how important it is to have "shopped" the store and the competitors before making that big presentation to the important buyer. Whether it is a national account or a local retailer, helping the retailer improve their offer for their Customers (and make more money) is the ONLY thing that can put your product in their stores.

41. The Decline and Fall of the Regional Mall

Who has not spent time in a mall; as a kid growing up, during the Holiday season to see all the wonderful décor, when the glamorous new store opens with all the fanfare? Enjoy it while you can, because it is quickly changing.

The first American Regional Mall as we know it, with a couple of anchor department stores (at least), two stories of shops (at least) and a food court, was completed in October of 1956, in suburban Minneapolis. It is called Southdale. Even the first mall had a compass point name.

What made the mall concept work was multi-fold. Easy freeway access. Large, available real estate with parking lots. Retailers willing to add store count by generally copying other examples of their stores creating a "chain" of similar stores. And of course willing consumers living in suburbs instead of cities.

With the U.S. highway expansion from the 50s-70s, these malls were where America shopped. If you live in a snow climate and can spend Saturday indoors, shopping, hanging out, enjoying the fresh architecture, maybe a performance indoors, see Santa and all the decorations at Christmas, who would not prefer that over the "downtown" experience; especially since you have moved to the suburbs to get away from the downtown. It was as though the retailers were coming to meet you.

Ironically, in many areas of the U.S., the mall was generally there first. At that point, housing developers had the attractiveness they needed to be able to sell (populate) a few thousand homes by offering all the conveniences of wherever you were in the city, out in the suburbs.

That was then. The United States has not built one of these types of suburban enclosed malls since 2006. Numbers vary by the various definitions, but somewhere between 1200 to 2000 total malls of this type existed in the prime through the 1990s.

However, the shopper has changed. In my opinion, the decline of the mall was driven by the same homogeneity that has caused many declines in the last 20 years. Creating scale, that is, to simply expand on something that is working and replicate it most certainly builds volume. But, the long term sustainability is missing – diversity. A variety of consumers with a variety of economic abilities and a variety of wants and needs.

As wonderful as these malls are or were, the re-purposing of their reason to exist tells the story. One third of these malls have vacancy rates at 25% or higher. At least 100 have been completely torn down. Many have added doctor's offices, gyms, and other space intensive services to back-fill the exodus of retailers capable of paying the increasingly expensive rents.

In Denver, 8 of the 13 regional malls are slated for redevelopment of some sort or other. One of these in Lakewood was converted from the typical 100 acres of centralized building and asphalt parking lot into..............wait for it............22 city style blocks of mixed use housing and retail. It kind of sounds like a downtown, doesn't it!! In fact, the city of Voorhees, NJ, tore down half of a mall and put their City Hall in the remainder.

Now coming to the mall near you….. City Hall!!

Most people have long forgotten or never heard of Dayton, Hudson, Emporium, Bullock's, May Company, Abraham and Strauss, J.W. Robinson, Hecht's, John Wanamaker's, Marshall-Fields, The Bon Marche, Burdine's (mostly all acquired by Macy's) which now live on in downtowns by the names etched in stone on still standing city landmark buildings across America. The malls, however, may or may not survive. The mall was not testimony to an entrepreneur's merchant-ability earned over the long haul through great service to the local population. The malls will instead be destroyed or transformed as the testimony to pure transactional commerce they turned out to be. To quote a mall executive, "We're Not Overbuilt, We're Under-Demolished". Maybe they can all become new "lifestyle centers" like Lakewood. One can only hope. For pictures of Abandoned Malls, go to www.DeadMalls.com.

42. You have to Ask More Questions!!

It is amazing how easy it is to ask and how often it is that people do not.

You can't get what you want for your business until you learn to ask. Period. Waiting for the generosity of others puts your business at the mercy of others. If you know what you want, ask for it. If you don't know what you want, ask questions to help you find out what you want.

Start with the easy stuff; How many would you like? When would you like it to arrive? When will you place the order?

Once you have trained yourself to ask the easy questions, graduate to the insightful stuff: How often do you buy these? What would your reorders look like? How can we help you sell the product? What can I do to make our relationship better?

Once you master those questions, start asking the graduate program questions: How big is the category for your stores? What products are you missing in this area? What would the price point be for that product?

No matter whether you are working with vendors, customers, staff, funding, whomever, everything is driven by what you ask. If you don't ask, don't be surprised when what you wanted does not come about. Business is not a restaurant with a menu of options.

Think of needing better payment terms; "where would our relationship need to be to get my business the very best terms/rates your company offers?"

With Retail Customers; "How well does this category do for your store now?" or "What type of sales volume per store in pieces do you see from this product per week?"

It's not just in person. Think of your website. Are you politely and artfully asking people if they would like to buy, everywhere at your website? Or are you providing a virtual Wikipedia experience (which by the way is FREE) all about your product with no call to action. When you're in a store, this is why the PRICE tag is on the products and why the checkstand is prominently visible from wherever you are in the store.

For your business to thrive, know what you want, know what you need to find out and then go out and ask all the questions you need to in order to make it happen.

The art of the ask is to always, always, always be aware of the motivation of the other party to provide on the ask. The more context awareness you have, the greater the likelihood the answer to your ask will be exactly what you want/need. Don't fool yourself into believing that you already "know" the answer. You know how the existing relationships got to where they are? You know, the existing relationships you are trying to break or at least modify! They asked for it.

The world revolves around what we ask for, not the offer.............the ask. The business people with the most thoughtful approach to asking for what they want almost always succeed. Rule #1 for all sales people – ASK for the order. Rule #1 for all business people – ASK for what you want.

43. Be relevant to the buyer

Every retailer fundamentally has 5 pillars to how they position themselves which in turn generates their traffic – Location, customers, product mix, service and price. In order to influence the buyer of a retailer, the seller must understand what the store will or will not be interested in investing in with its inventory dollars in order to serve the traffic the store creates.

Of the five elements each has a unique opportunity for the seller to address depending on the product they are offering.

Location is a good topic to bring up if the store is located in a geographically advantaged position. Selling books or magazines in an airport, selling sandwiches near a park, selling greeting cards in a hospital come to mind. The seller can't change the location of the business, but, they can frame their product as appropriate given the location that exists.

Customers is a wonderful topic to discuss. If a store caters to young people, which can be determined from overall product mix, color schemes, background music and a host of other cues, talking about how that audience is the target segment for your products is very smart. Not all stores sell to all comers by virtue of how friendly they make their space to a particular audience. Be aware and take note so you can identify that in your conversation.

Product mix is a large way retailers create or turn away segments of the community. A convenience store is not a grocery store. Small or limited sizes or narrow selections within a product range can make shopping easier for those that are so inclined, but, will turn away customers seeking a particular brand or who want the better value of larger sizing. Be sure to discuss why your product belongs in the existing product mix.

Service is a mixed bag. From assisted to unassisted stores, be sure you understand what the view from your buyer's perspective is on her store's enthusiasm for Consumer/Staff interaction. Play up your product's fit into exactly that notion by calling out the pros of the package or the ease of understanding for both staff and consumers.

Price is a large determinant of the store traffic, but, is not a stand alone element. Low prices generally mean lower margins per transaction and therefore require higher traffic. The higher the traffic, the more throughput at the checkout becomes more important than service in the aisles. Keeping shelves stocked takes on a high priority. If your product targets toward or away from these environments, talk about it and talk about why.

Continually evaluate the buyer's interaction and response to your statements. If your conversation is largely you talking, that's a bad sign. A conversation is both parties talking. A presentation is one person talking. Always remember that a buyer has other issues to consider besides what you see to be a great fit. Your product may actually NOT fit today, and may fit next month or next quarter.

44. Email does not equal a conversation

All the time I am confronted with frustrated people because someone has not "responded" to their email. All the time I ask if they have called them to follow-up. Most of the time, the answer is no.

The top priority in business is to create relationships. In order to do that, one must have conversations. Email is terrible at creating conversations. Email is chunks of dialogue thrust at a recipient to be read as time and priority allow and maybe create a response. It is not a substitute for two people talking through topics on the phone any more than a text message is the same as email.

So I suggest everyone consider appreciating this hierarchy of communications:

Top Level: Face to Face. You can't beat it. Use Skype or whatever, but, always work toward this. It engages three senses and a dimension; sight, sound and touch (shaking hands, writing notes, etc.) and time.

Phone call: the next best thing to being there. It engages only one sense, sound, and retains the dimension of time.

Voice mail: retains the sense of sound but loses the dimension of time.

Email: Only engages sight and loses the dimension of time.

Everything else: worse.

When you want to get to a buyer or you want to step into someone's space, you don't want your very important message to be seen "at the recipient's convenience" and seen through pixels. Be willing to pursue via phone calls or whatever else is needed to have a "meeting".

If all you want to do is provide background, follow-up, write a letter, etc., sure, use email. But, it's incredible to me that a sales person would send an email sales presentation, wait for a response, and then be surprised that their product, which is a perfect fit, is rejected.

In essence, the effort to get into that store was so unimportant to the seller, that they delegated it to the poorest communication model possible (albeit very efficient), email. If it's important, if you want it to happen, if it means something to you, then get the person in a room or on the phone. Otherwise, your effort is just part of the daily noise that shows up in a computer. Does it take more time? Of course, that's the point. Where you put your time is where you get results and how you grow your business.

45. What does a distributor do in the wholesale to retail trade?

Many folks have a belief that a distributor, that has sales people, will be all that is required to put products into retail stores. Nothing could be farther from the truth.

First, the role of a distributor; A distributor provides a relatively seamless method to flow products both electronically and physically into a retail chain without the retailer needing to setup a new vendor. It reduces the retailer risk of shipment mistakes. It also allows the retailer to place orders from assorted brands through one vendor on a more frequent basis. The retailer then places one much larger order with the distributor, consolidating lots of vendors into one shipment and then one invoice and one payment – to the distributor.

Depending on the retail channel, the distributor buys products from the brand at 5-30% discount off of the wholesale price on the products it purchases from the vendor which allows it to match the wholesale price to the retailer.

Even though the distributor has a team of people called sales people, that should not be mistaken for a team of salespeople out promoting your product. The primary responsibility of the distributor sales person is relationship management; the relationship between the retailer and the distributor. What that comes down to is making sure the retailer is continually satisfied with the performance of the distributor and the EXISTING items in the store.

What is generally lost on a new vendor is that there are hundreds of vendors and thousands of products already in the distributor's product range, with many of them already in the retailer's store. In order to place your new product in the store, space may need to be taken from some other product already on the shelf. Retail is a zero sum proposition, that is, the store is already full of products so to add yours requires something else to be bumped.

What should it be? The distributor wants it to be some other distributor's product, but, not their own product.

The distributor's fear is that what is bumped is something else the distributor is already selling. In that case, your "new sale" is the distributor's "lost sale" replaced by your "new sale". That equals no growth in sales for the distributor (unless the price is higher or the sales volume is greater).

In the end, the primary way a vendor gets product into stores is by selling it to them, through sales people or directly. That does not mean that the vendor will ship it to the retailer (which is determined by the retailer), or that it will invoice the retailer, only that the "deal" was made by the vendor. This effort is called placement and it is almost entirely up to you to get it. The distributors are not in the "deal" making business, nor are they typically very effective at initial placement. To tell the story of the brand or product there is no substitute for the vendor or the vendor's sales person. To get shipments to the store and service the needs of the retailer after placement, that's the distributor's role at which they are very good.

It's painful to think that the sales people are not really selling. But, thinking of it differently, once your product is in the store, thanks to your sales efforts, the sales people of the distributor will be charged with keeping your space. If you can get it in, the distributor will work to keep it in.

46. Why distributors are not Plan A to get into U.S. retailers

There is a common misperception in the marketplace from newer entrepreneurs that getting distributors is the key to success. It becomes the Plan A as evidenced by the number of websites that post "distributors wanted" or the equivalent on their pages.

The role of distributors in the U.S. is not like that of the role of a distributor in almost the entire rest of the world. Distributors in the U.S. are by and large completely on the supply side of the path to retailers. That is to say, they do not create demand from retailers, nor are they very good at placement of new brands.

Why should they be? Their model is built around warehouses full of tens of thousands of SKUs for which they earn revenues based on inventory turns of SKUs, not the passionate pursuit of consumers for the amazing product they have created.

I always counsel that the distributor is only going to be successful to the degree the brand is willing to invest in creating retailer demand. There are numerous resources out there to learn how to be good at selling to retailers. Retailers are also not in the passionate pursuit of consumers for what they have created. The distributor only needs to ensure that they will generate revenues with <u>whatever</u> merchandise they put on their shelves.

Generating demand from retailers may require generating demand from consumers, or partnering with stores for POS messaging and/or marketing campaigns that will push the recognition or interest of the solution – drive traffic. It's always about more than just your wonderful product.

Plan A should always be to reach out to retailers first (or contract/hire sales people to do it). Get them interested in carrying the product. They will tell you who the distributor is they need the brand to utilize to make the fulfillment work. Then contact the distributor who will be a motivated partner in the relationship. Distributors are not placement machines. They manage and maintain relationships with retailers. Some are better than others. Don't get caught thinking distributors are Plan A when you have not invested in the work to create demand from retailers. When money matters (when does it not?), if there is no demand, there is no incentive for anyone to move forward.

47. An empty shelf space generates no revenue

The greatest risk a retailer faces is an empty shelf space on their sales floor. Paying rent for empty shelf space is not a success strategy for retailers. Even slow selling product on a shelf is earning some revenue, but, no stock on the shelf earns a big goose egg every time.

Therefore, the greatest risk to a retailer is to be aligned with a vendor that does not deliver as promised, delivers late, ships short or does anything else that is not going to keep the shelves full with product. Fail to execute and the retailer is left with all the risk.

What if there was punishment for vendors that do not meet their delivery obligations (who do not execute on time and to the letter)? In the consumer product landscape there are punishments, and they can be very, very painful (read

58

expensive). They are called chargebacks, where a retailer charges back a fixed amount for the missed delivery from the payment it makes for the invoice.

Yet, these oversights are so common for vendors that the retail industry has setup chargeback systems to penalize vendors for not meeting the delivery expectation established by the retailer and agreed to by the vendor. One of the many ways a new vendor can fail. Fail to execute and you may fail entirely.

One department store retailer deducts 5% per week of the Purchase Order value from its eventual payment to the vendor for late delivery. Another electronics retailer submits all orders with a "Cancel if not delivered by" on all Purchase Orders. When a shipment arrives late, it is sent back. The entire consumer product industry won't take new product into stores in December. And, this one is easy, there is no way a college book store can have product arrive after the back to school rush is over.

The lesson….read the Vendor Guide to be absolutely certain you can deliver to the letter, unless you are willing to suffer the consequences of elimination as a vendor. Harsh – you bet. There is a long line of other vendors with other fascinating items that can go in that empty space on the shelf. Remember, it's all about filling the shelf space in the store.

Flawless execution receives the reward of getting paid. Perform or perish.

48. Tradeshow Success Secrets from a Tradeshow Veteran

Look at the top person in any live performance field like entertainers or athletes. Now envision what that person must do every day to stay in condition to be successful. Every one of them works for "me, incorporated" which means they need to constantly work to enhance their reputation to increase their income. We only see the few moments or hours they are "on", but, that is far, far from the extent of their preparation to be ready to be "on" at any given time.

The trade show is the commercial equivalent of live performance. For consumer products, trade shows are often a hefty piece of the annual marketing spend. There is no substitute for taking your showroom on the road and setting it up to be seen by attendees who's job title is "buyer". When you have 60 different conversations each day for 3 or 4 days, it is a grueling schedule.

Having performed in well over 100 shows, there is a very short list of things that make a Show experience terrific or outstanding, that will put you at the top of your game, that surprisingly few exhibitors discuss or follow. To be a peak performer in this environment is to embrace all 8 of my Rules for Tradeshow Success.

Every company has a design idea about what they can do to get the people in the aisle to look at their booth, walk in and interact. For the thousands of dollars you will be spending on shows, let me take a very quick moment to provide my 8 Rules for Tradeshow Success that you can do to make yourself unique in the sea of "competitors". Once you have committed to following these 8 Rules, **THEN** spend the tens of thousands of dollars on your space, the exhibit, drayage, shipping, furniture, floor covering, electricity, apps, hotels, food, transportation and whatever else you're doing, Miss any of these 8 Rules and you may very well waste every penny.

Before the Show:

1. Send an invitation to anyone you might know before the show. – Email is free. Email everyone at least twice prior to the show. Send them a thoughtful "looking forward to seeing you" or "please stop by". An invitation to visit for a thoughtful purpose is far more valuable than a promotional message.

2. Have a strategy for why you are at the show and define your successful outcome and know how to achieve it. – Show up to tell a story. Know the story and tell it all the time. Tell the why. Even if you go to the same show every year and are only showing your newest products, tell people why they exist and why they should care. Don't just lead people in and ask them "what do you think".

3. Don't expect a show to be only about "orders". – Shows are one more opportunity for relationship progression. Know what you want to achieve in advance. If Big Opportunity buyer is in your booth, they are unlikely to pull out a Purchase Order, but, that does not make their visit a failure. Make the time valuable for both of you by learning about them and their business and sharing about your business. Have a conversation!

At the Show:

4. Be rested and eat well, every day. – This is so often overlooked. Staying out late because you're in Las Vegas will cost you the next day. Skipping breakfast or lunch or drinking dinner will only make you less sharp. You can't afford to be any less sharp than the person in the last booth the buyer visited.

5. Show up on time and stay until the end. – The time pressed buyers (the busy ones that you want to meet) are there at the door before the start and stay on the floor until the end. That means you want to be there when they are. You want to be just as fresh about your product as they are about their business and what they are interested in discussing.

6. Take notes. – Come back home with a clear awareness of what each contact discussed and what the next step is. Write on the cards. Take a notepad. Do something that indicates you will follow through. It is not the buyer's responsibility to contact you if you want their business. It's yours.

7. Qualify everyone you meet so you can focus on the ones that matter. – Know the types of attendees and how to know who is who. A "buyer" from Big Opportunity is in your booth and they are only the assistant to the assistant in the wrong department, or worse for you, work in a store. Learn what you can and move them on.

After the Show:

8. Absolutely, no matter what, make sure everyone you made a commitment to contact gets contacted.

– By the end of the 72 hours after a show, make sure every contact you have has received an email "thank you" and you've set a time frame for meaningful followup on whatever you discussed. If it's just send a catalog, then do it. If it's going to take a week, tell them.

Face time with buyers is the most valuable opportunity you can ever achieve. Do absolutely everything to maximize your chances of having lots of highly meaningful engagements at every show by following these simple Tradeshow Success rules.

49. Your Brand's top 5 Prospects – who are they?

It is very easy, when the landscape contains hundreds of possible retail outlets, to think that all you need to do is get out there and the right retailers will find you. That thinking has cost many a startup and even seasoned pros incredibly priceless calendar time working with all the wrong retailers for all the seemingly right reasons.

If you can't answer this question you are already in trouble: "Who are my top 5 prospects in every retail channel and what are we doing to get our product in their stores?"

Any salesperson worth a nickel knows who their most important prospects are they are targeting to grow their income. They put in a healthy percentage of their effort doing what they can to get in front of those buyers. They may call every single day, multiple times, leaving messages or not, in the hope that the buyer will answer the phone (which by the way is most common between 8-9am and 4-5pm their local time).

First they may need to get the phone number and buyer's name. Once they have a phone number and a buyer's name, what else do you need? Contact.

Yet, amazingly, most business owners don't even have the names of the top 5 retail targets, let alone the names of the buyers and the phone number to contact them.

If you want your product in the store badly enough, do whatever it takes to get the buyer's attention and make them aware of your product. Know their business. Know your rationale. Know your marketplace AND MAKE CONTACT.

If you don't know who your top 5 prospects are, know their business, know your rationale and know your marketplace, that is why you are already in growth trouble. Then by all means, spend tons of dollars and time at trade shows crossing your fingers that retailers important to your business might walk by. It's your money and your time. Focus, focus, focus.

50. Buyer fatigue – How to avoid it in the initial meeting

Every person has a patience level with every business meeting as to how much time to invest to serve their needs. Buyers are no different. They willingly invest as much time as they deem a product or relationship will need to determine or advance the value that relationship adds to their efforts. Additionally, buyers are always aware that the less time for the biggest bang is the goal.

In that reality in your initial meeting, you can not expect buyers to willingly give your 1 SKU or 30 SKU product 45 minutes to hear all about the beginnings of the company, the details of how it is made and the thoughtfulness you have put into each and every product. Not in the first meeting anyway.

To avoid buyer fatigue, your first mission with a buyer is to simplify your business and product range to exactly what will get them to understand it in very little time AND make them want to hear more. Keep in mind, in the store, the consumer will spend less than 8 seconds looking at your packaged product and making a "touch it" or "move-on" decision. Retail buyers will give you more than 8 seconds, but not much more. Here is a formula for avoiding Buyer Fatigue.

Boil down your initial over-arching presentation to 2-3 minutes on why you exist and why this particular buyer should care. (Secret insight – it's about making money for the store.)

Presuming you can get enough interest for them to stick with you on why you exist, it's time to distill your product range down to the most compelling items. At this point, most people then launch into why the product is so cool for the consumer and travel down a dirt road full of pot holes. Don't go there. Instead pick the 3 topmost reasons you are in business and then choose the 3 best examples of those reasons as expressed in your product range AND how the consumer will discover those same elements when the product is on the shelf or in their hands. Reinforce your story through your products. The products are an extension of the business.

Ten minutes – tops for 3 products. That's 15 minutes total.

You're saying "wait I have 20 products and I can't get it all done in just 15 minutes". And therein lies my point. If the buyer isn't enthusiastic to continue after 15 minutes, you haven't made the compelling presentation. A TED talk is 15 minutes – OR LESS. The buyer will check out. And there you have the initial meeting version of buyer fatigue.

If I am a buyer, I am exclusively thinking about the connection between your presentation and what the consumer will see in the store when they look at the packaged product. The greater the connection between your presentation and the packaged product, the more enthusiastic the buyer becomes.

Use the first 5 minutes to frame and define your Company. Use 10 minutes to call attention to products that define the entire range – "if you get these, you'll get everything else". Use the rest of whatever time the buyer allows you to be about the buyer and what the buyer wants to talk about.

Running through a catalog, doing product demos, putting out 20 more SKUs, that may or may not be necessary, but, should never be assumed to BE the presentation. Show and tell is what kids do in the classroom. Show and tell should not be how you start a long lasting mutually beneficial professional relationship.

Your Path to Consumers

51. Know, Like, Trust: it can be that easy

What I enjoy most about being in consumer products is that even if I'm not the target market for a product, I am a consumer, so at least I have an idea of how a consumer thinks. I can look at a product with the eye of the target market and evaluate it based on the vantage point of that person.

To do that in a store or online requires a certain pathway not at all unlike developing a new friendship. It is now called "know, like, trust".

I don't know what the old way was called; build it they will come? Advertise until you run out of money? Whatever it was called, the world wide web has changed everything.....or has it?

The concept of having a business relationship used to be very much under the control and influence of the seller (the store or the service provider). They would send out ongoing messages "buy me, buy me, buy me". The more messages, the more buying. MBAs ruled the world.

Now, a lot has changed. Own a restaurant and provide bad service, Yelp reviews will punish you. Own a hotel and miss a turndown and Travelocity reviews will punish you. Examples go on and on. But, who's extolling the punishment – yep, the consumer.

Consumers run the world. They do homework. They make some sort of effort to get to know what they are doing. (I think we always did.) The seller must then make an effort to become known, not by "buy me, buy me, buy me", but, by the deeds, actions and activities of the business.

As it turns out, if I know you by your deeds, I might begin to like you. How? We've all had personal relationships. There shouldn't be a mystery here. You be considerate, be thoughtful, be respectful, let other people talk (everything your mom told you), etc. If you do all that, maybe, just maybe someone will trust you with money (OMG, not money!!) to take care of a personal need or want with your product.

The Yellow pages are disappearing, because phoning a stranger with a problem you need solved is only for emergencies. Otherwise, I'm going to my network. Ask a friend. Facebook. Linked In. Rotary. Colleagues. Start there.

Know, like, trust, isn't exactly new. When I was a kid we knew the people at the grocery store. We knew the people at the local shoe store. The manager of the bank was my friend's dad. We knew the people at the drug store. But, those were all locally owned businesses.

Maybe know, like, trust is just a recycle of a retro perspective that we did not realize we had lost. By corporatizing America, which has been great for many, we have also de-personalized many, many experiences into just transactions. What know, like, trust says to me is that the consumer is looking for businesses focused on being real with people again. In a small town that happens more. In a big city, less so.

On the web, not at all. Except...............through social media. Be considerate, be thoughtful, be respectful, let other people talk. It's harder than it sounds.

52. Know, Like, Trust: Part 2 - It's all up to the Consumer

Have you ever seen The Music Man by Meredith Willson? The story takes place in 1912 River City, Iowa. It's about a traveling musical instrument salesman who's job it is to sell band instruments to the the locals for cash and then move on before the instruments arrive. Why move on? Because eventually the buyers will find out that without any music teacher, the new owners will never learn how to play their instruments. The seller, Mr. Harold Hill, knows the buyers will be angry with him and want their money back. The first piece of music in the musical is a conversation among assorted sales people on a train and carries the line "but you gotta know the territory".

So what has changed in the "territory" 100 years since? The internet. You could call it the Consumer Declaration of Independence, because the fact that consumers can now see dozens, scores or even hundreds of "reviews" of the experiences of other consumers, the buyer no longer has the ability to present a picture that can not turn out to be real (like Mr. Hill could).

That makes the consumer (buyer) king in ways never before imagined. If you watch Kitchen Nightmares or Hotel Impossible or Restaurant Impossible (where the show ends with a call to action for restaurateurs: if you own a failing restaurant......), then you can see just how many people that own consumer businesses, are clueless about the customer experience in their own establishment; or worse, are aware of the overall displeasure and choose to consider it the fault of the consumer and not their business. The consumer then votes with their money and their reviews et voila, it's a TV show about your failing business. And by the way, you may lose your house if your business fails. That's a wake up call.

The consumer now has insights through all these new channels; Yelp, Travelocity, Amazon, AirBnB, etc. that we all read and pay attention to. If you're going to buy it anyway, you take the positive reviews. If you were on the fence, you're open to input. If you didn't want to buy it in the first place, you accept all the negative reviews.

Try to imagine 20 years ago and staying in a stranger's home via AirBnB without the reviews of the previous guests?

We, the Consumers control whether we want to know, like or trust everyone. The corporations and stores no longer do. No fooling around. No slight of hand. We can back test every claim via the internet. We can look it up. Whatever experience you seek, you can find it. Mr. Hill can no longer do what he did in the last town, selling instruments no one will learn how to play. We, the Consumer have won an unexpected Revolutionary War thanks to the internet. And not a single shot was fired, although the business carnage is everywhere over the last 20 years.

53. Amazon can not be your company standard

Just because Amazon can ship stuff via a no-freight buy-in program and get it to you in two days (soon to be delivered by drones?), does not make that the market standard you should strive to achieve.

Amazon has spent billions of dollars to get where it is. The investments in technology and distribution power are off the charts. You have likely never spoken to someone at Amazon who knew anything about what you called about. Who even calls Amazon???

Here is what to do to be indifferent to Amazon and not feel trapped by the Amazon expectation:

- When a Customer orders at your website (or even your Amazon store), they get a thoughtful, friendly auto response receipt that sets their expectation for delivery and subsequent performance.
- Include a phone number at your website and certainly on your receipt for them to call.
- Make crystal clear promises you are certain to be able to achieve all the time (ships in 5 days, not ships tomorrow).
- In the shipment you send, say thank you and indicate what to do if they are not happy.

The people buying at your website (or even your Amazon store) are buying from you because you are NOT Amazon. Don't pretend you are. That only makes it worse. Make your responses thoughtful and human and be sure to give them all they might want if they were standing right in front of you making the special purchase they hunted down, because, that is exactly what they did. Your reputation is riding on it.

54. Why drop shipping will kill your business

It is counter intuitive to think that offering added services to certain retailers in order to gain their business is not a valuable thing to do. With many new businesses, it is almost mandatory that they do something above and beyond simply selling products wholesale to retailers. Case in point, when an etailer asks you drop ship to their Customers.

The internet has changed a lot of the ways brands sell to consumers. Many brands have created hybrid versions of themselves in which they wear a retailer hat at their own website and a wholesale hat in the broader marketplace selling to retailers. Some brands offer links at websites to retailers. Some don't.

Creating B2C relationships is an overwhelming temptation. It can appear as a no-brainer with significantly higher margins and direct contact with avid consumers. If you have experienced a crowd-funding campaign, ever toured Zappo's or been directly involved in consumer direct sales, as I have, you come to appreciate just how much work there is involved in taking care of consumers.

No matter how attractive the margins, no one accounts for buyer remorse return rates which can easily run up to 15%, which is a deep cut in the overall sales, let alone the added work that returns create as negative sales.

But, presuming you are OK with all that work because you think it will create visibility, and you are OK with competing with your own retailers, when an etailer asks you to drop ship using their UPS account and they still want the wholesale price, you absolutely should scratch your head and say "why"?

The economics are universally terrible. You are doing the same fulfillment work as a retailer, and only getting the wholesale price, one piece at a time. Worse, most of the time you can't even put in your own marketing materials. Instead of shipping to a retailer or etailer that will actually take ownership and pay you for 100 pieces, an online store is going to market your products, see if they sell, and dribble the orders to you one at a time. Likely they will want fast turnaround and tracking information, too, thereby requiring almost the same amount of infrastructure as a B2C business at half the sales value and a greater percentage reduction of gross margin.

Don't do it. The temptress of capability and revenue growth must be tempered by the actual costs of drop shipping products to consumers and all the transactional effort entailed to make the effort work. Then there are the returns! And I'm not even talking about the massive distraction it is from your wholesale business.

If you have older product you need to get out of, do what you have to do. When you have front line product and you have chosen to be a wholesale brand, be a wholesale brand. As soon as you try to be all things on all platforms to all etailers, you have set a course for reduced profits and increased headaches. There are plenty of places to sell your products. Find those outlets that are your annuity partners, ordering and reordering, taking their appropriate percentage of the sale commensurate for their risk (inventory) and work (customer service). Most importantly, always remember just because you **can** ship one piece at a time, almost never means you **should** ship one piece at a time. It's an entirely different equation.

55. Do Consumers matter to a wholesale brand?

Once your business transitions from your consumer direct, proof of concept phase (crowdfunding, holiday fairs, etc.) and you make the leap to becoming a wholesale supplier – whether you like it or not – your business immediately transforms into one that is expected to make money for others with your products. This transition happens because you have made the decision to build an organization where everyone gets compensated for their roles to grow the organization.

Many think of an "organization" as a group of people who all work for one enterprise. But, that's not the case at all. In automobiles, the independent dealerships with mechanics and sales people, who buy and sell Honda cars are part of the Honda organization. In cosmetics, the independent representatives who buy and sell Avon are part of the Avon organization. In soft drinks, all of the bottling companies with delivery drivers, sales people and bottling plant staffs that sell Coca Cola products are part of the Coke organization.

The fact that all these entities are "independent" has nothing to do with the fact that they are part of larger organization. Therefore, the moment you commit to the path of wholesale, you forever change your relationship with the consumer because you now "share" that consumer relationship with others.

Like bees to flowers, you still need to make your offer to the consumer as attractive as possible. Once accomplished through proof of concept, your primary wholesale responsibility is to ensure that everyone in your organization is making money. Whether that is retailers who stock and sell your products, sales reps who sell to retailers or distributors and their infrastructure that sells to retailers. All of them are participants in your organization.

As these entities in your organization succeed, you succeed. To the degree you have made a great product, effectively packaged that sells through in stores (generally without any assistance) you are awesome. To the degree that the product gets bottom shelf placement or never gets into a sales meeting between sales people and buyers, you will fail. Not because your product isn't fantastic, but, because no one is making any money with your product. Everyone's relationship with your Company is predicated on MAKING MONEY.

Focusing on where your organization makes money is the responsible thing to do as a wholesale brand. Your successful wholesale organization is counting on you to show them how to make money with your products, which, by the way, is nothing at all like showing them how great your products are. And that's the distinction that separates the long term successes from the flashes in the pan. Because there will always be competitors.

56. This one time offer for new Customers; Misguided gratitude

Have you ever seen those "new customer" offers? All the media companies do it; satellite TV, phones, etc. Buy now and get the first month free. Buy now and....... Ever ask yourself why you would give a "new customer" the impression that they are only going to get your "best offer" when they are new, which means later, when they are your long time loyal customer, they will be treated like commoners?

Why would any business be so disrespectful to loyal customers and gracious to strangers?

That's the upside down part of some marketing strategies – always treat strangers well, but, be indifferent to those that you know and who have made a commitment to work together.

Make a personal commitment to treat your existing, loyal customers (the consumers or the retailers) with the respect they deserve (the choir). These people and their businesses are the ones funding your business. Make them feel wanted.

Give them things, like the most important words in any language – Thank you (Mahalo, Merci, Gracias, etc.). And don't just say it. Show it!

How?

That's the most fun part – surprise them. Display your gratitude. Impress them. Delight them. Give them your time. Give them your best thoughts. Give them greater access to you or something they really would like. Whatever it is, make it personal. You and your business are a MEDIA company. Use it.

Show your gratitude to your best Customers and they will be loyal. Invest in strangers to make them Customers and they will be transitory. If you want a business that is built on always needing to have new customers to achieve growth (which is really expensive), treat strangers great and ignore loyalty. If you want to build a strong community of repeat customers, once they come into your business, overwhelm them with gratitude in whatever creative ways you can dream up.

Find your core audience and then lavish them. Your business will reward you in direct proportion to your creativity in getting people to be delighted that you are thinking about them and are grateful for their business.

57. The marketing troika

This is my definition of marketing, gathered from owning and working for multiple consumer product brands, selling into 1000s of doors, on multiple continents, over the course of 30 years.

Marketing is the messaging that is developed to portray a business, product or offer, which is put into locations (virtual or otherwise) where that message will be seen by people who are in the right time in a decision making process to allow the message to penetrate their shields. Right message, right place, right time.

For marketing to work well, it has to meet all three criteria, a troika. It has to be an appropriate message, delivered in the right place, delivered at the right time. If any of these three areas are a miss, the marketing effort is likely to underperform the intended outcome.

From this starting point, every single marketing effort has to begin with a strategy that starts with who is the audience, From that humble beginning comes how to convey to an audience an appropriate message at the right place and the right timing so as to achieve the outcome desired for the business.

Start there, all the time. Never get into any marketing efforts where the troika has not been considered at the outset. Just because someone else has effective marketing in some way does not mean you will, too. Good marketing must take into account the audience, their mindset, their needs/wants, where and when they are most likely to appreciate having the message introduced to them.

A great message at the wrong time is useless. Great timing with a bad location is useless. Great locations with a poor message is useless (like lots of websites or trade show booths). Whether it is the website you create, the emailing you send out, the banner ads you post online, the presentation you make at a trade show, or the effort you make in social media, go through the same process every time and your effectiveness will skyrocket.

58. Marketing: Stop Guessing

Here are two marketing choices: Send out messages and communications based on what you think people want to hear or should hear about your product or service OR send out messages and communications based on what people have told you they want to hear and will respond to.

Is that a stumper? Not to me. Here's the deal; if you have even only 20 customers, ask them what they value and what they want?

A lot of companies make market feedback into some sort of ordeal. Survey Monkey and other internet tools have made the ability to create a survey and send it to gobs of strangers or even customers pretty easy. Does that mean they care and will really give you valuable information? Does it mean you're even asking the right questions. No, it does not.

I've watched these things be created, even created my own. They are generated internally with the best of "affirmation" intentions. That is, "how are we doing within these confines". On a 1-10 scale please rate our (fill it in). Please select the answer that best states how you think we (fill it in). I hate these things, don't you? This creates a whole bunch of data points, which the marketing firm always tells you are exactly what you want.

You know what, I'm not so sure.

Here is a new and fresh approach in a time crunched world where we know for fact we don't know what is on the mind of the other person. How about we just ask them these three simple questions:

1. What is the greatest value you get from us?

2. What is the most important thing you get from our relationship?

3. What is one thing we could do that we are not currently doing?

I would rather have 20 of these answers than 4000 data points in some Harris Poll type of format. From this I would fully understand what are the most valuable and important things we do. I would know exactly what the existing audience would like to see us do to go further or how to get more prospects that have the same perspective as our existing Customers.

Once past these three questions I would ask two more:

1. What are your goals for the upcoming _____?

2. What will stop you from achieving those goals?

Try it. Ask folks on the phone. Keep track. Ask them in an email. Maybe one question at a time. However you choose to do it – ASK. We all know in sales you have to ask. What if that is the simplest way to look at marketing, too.

Of course, then you need to be willing to listen to the answers. Special thanks to Steve Napolitan for making this so simple.

59. Do Likes matter?

Over time I have had many conversations with entrepreneurs enamored with the number of Likes that they are able to acquire online. Whether a lot of Likes or a few Likes is a good thing is almost completely dependent on the strategy in place to convert Likes to revenues in some way in the future.

Here is a metaphor for Likes. Plan to throw a party and publish it in your community online and to your friends. A few people you have never met from your community will come to your party for the free food or drinks. Lots of your actual friends come. They all hang out. They like or don't like the vibe or the other guests. Eventually everyone leaves. How many of those new guests become your new friends? Friends in that they are someone you want to know, are glad they are there and have a mutual respect and engagement together? How many of those guests simply said thank you and told you how much they enjoyed the party?

Likes online are the same as those guests who may have thanked you. They may be people who just came and went who had a good time. They say in effect, I like how you did this and I might want to be a peripheral part of it. Then what happens for them? If you do nothing except hold another party in a few days, weeks or months, which is what most entrepreneurs do online, you will continue to put more and more money into holding parties with no return on that investment except becoming good at producing parties and meeting people who like to attend parties.

What do Likes need to have to determine if they are Likes that matter? A next step. A call to action. A progression to an ongoing deeper relationship, almost certainly on a path to revenue production for your company. The entrepreneurs who know how to turn Likes into loyal followers who make financial (buy your stuff) or time commitments (promote your stuff) to the company, they get it. To the rest, a Like is largely just a button that someone spontaneously pushed to show support for the effort. Sort of like applause at the end of a performance. Gratitude, not participation.

At the performance we paid in advance. The applause equates to "thank you for providing a high quality value". For a Like we pay later, maybe. Develop a roadmap for how Likes can become more engaged than post performance applause. Likes must lead to revenues or the energy to create the Likes is simply an education or entertainment effort. That's the challenge.

60. Point of Sale is where decisions are made

Often I find myself reminding consumer product companies and brand managers of the critical importance of investing in Point of Sale support materials. In the U.S. 70% of decision making happens when the Customer is already in the store.

When we all go in stores and see the creative ways "the product" is getting more attention in the noise of the store, that should be a wake up call to how important this effort is. It's not just about "branding", it's about selling, right there, in that moment.

Visibility in every store is critical. Budgeting for signage, be it from the ceiling, on the hook, at the cash/wrap, shelf talkers, merchandise displays or some other creative method is required to make a product or brand sizzle.

If you have a breakthrough product or something new that has a story to tell or a reason to be or needs lifestyle connection, in order to win the day in the store, expand your thinking past "it's in" thinking that's all it takes. Go for gold and support the heck out of it and from inside the store. It IS EXACTLY what the store wants to achieve. The limit is only in your own creativity and exposure to what kinds of things are currently being done in the retail market place.

Which I guess is why I have to remind those brand managers and entrepreneurs, because, unfortunately, they don't go out shopping. If you're in consumer products, every trip to every store any day is called market research. To some, I suppose, it's still just called shopping and maybe something they don't want to do themselves. If you don't get into the landscape where your products are sold, you're not very likely to be able to find creative ways to beat the competition.

Getting in the store is only phase 1. Selling through the store – that's the magic. Winners create magic. Everyone else gets replaced in short order as an underperformer. The consumer is not looking for products – they crave the magic. Get into stores and create magic, or someone else will.

61. Packaging – May be more important than your product

Have you ever shopped for wine? Unless you do it a lot, the wine aisle is very difficult to shop. You may know what a Zinfandel tastes like, but, how do you choose among 50 different zinfandels at prices from under $10 to over $50. How do you know whether a $40 wine is 4 times as good as a $10 wine? How do you choose to buy the one you buy with no real way to know whether what is in the bottle will be good to you (I'm presuming everyone recognizes that everyone's tastes are different)?

Packaging!

And on a bottle of wine, that's not much space.

The only hope of the winemaker is to do the right job with the packaging to tell the story of what they want you to know or appreciate about their product which is inside the standard bottle.

Maybe the winemaker has a sense of humor and wants people to chuckle. Maybe the wine maker loves art and wants to appeal to others who recognize good art. Maybe the uniqueness of this wine is that it is from Arkansas.

Whatever the approach, the packaging needs to tell the story visually through visuals, graphics and text, that will convert a shopper of the zinfandel category into a buyer of their wine at the price they want/need to stay in business.

Whether it is the artwork, the fonts, the positioning, the color scheme, the message or any of a host of other attributes, if the overall package does not create a quick alignment with the shopper, there is no sale.

Given the critical nature of packaging for wines, there is an entire specialized niche of designers who have studied what is effective at converting shoppers into customers.

Unfortunately, many people new to consumer products hire a graphic designer. They know they need graphics and design. The most important way to convert shoppers into customers is left up to some friend of a friend who knows how to use

Adobe Illustrator. Some data shows that in some categories as high as 80% of decision making for what the consumer will buy is made IN THE STORE!

Here is the most important piece of advice I can ever offer – when it comes to packaging, hire an experienced consumer packaging designer. Do the homework needed to know your likely shelf space location. Know your packaging needs. Walk lots of retail stores looking only at packaging and see what works to get your attention and why. Learn how to communicate with your packaging designer to collaborate with them to get your product the absolute best design possible for the space you want to occupy.

When you do that, buyers will jump on your product right away, and if they do, so do consumers. In a retail store, to displace an incumbent of the space it already occupies (the store is full already), you need to be special and effective. Not one, but, both.

Most problems in sell through of product in a store stem from a great idea that is not portrayed well in the packaging. Success, as it was with creating your product, comes to those who do the homework and create the team that can best visually articulate the core message THE CONSUMER needs to see to be converted from a shopper to a customer. (Don't forget the goal of the package is to sell the product, not satisfy the ego of the designer or the founder.)

62. There are more to ways to reach a market than ever before

One of the very simple questions we ask entrepreneurs is where do you see your products? Not surprisingly, the most popular answers are Target and Apple. In many respects, this question helps us understand the thoroughness of the business developer's awareness of the market(s) in which they may find placement or opportunity for their products. Here's why:

Products come into the lives of all of us as consumers in lots of ways, not all of them even self driven. How many pens do you have that you purchased and how many just "showed up" or you got at the doctor's office or from your financial planner? How about shirts? You get the idea.

At CES, as an example, I was struck by the number of product ideas that are not needed to be driven by Best Buy or Apple. This arc of thinking asks questions about what is the frame of mind of the consumer when they come to the particular store (Apple for example). Although Apple sells its share of iPhone cases, my money says most consumers buy a new case when they see one they like, wherever that is, be it a drug store, auto store or Starbucks. It's only $10-25. For many an iPhone case is like jewelry for a phone.

With new electronic products coming out that are app connected, the locations to sell the device that creates the app connection could be huge. Walgreens, Safeway, Hobby Lobby, Pac Sun, Victoria Secret, etc. Any of these could be early partners for all kinds of really cool startup products. It may not be as prestigious to tell your friends, "I'm in Hobby Lobby", but, maybe it will make more money, and be in a much less competitive environment.

I won't even get into premium and promotional products. What if the product could go in a different direction altogether and be offered as an incentive for Customers at AMEX?

These questions would all be asked in a thorough "marketing plan". Unfortunately, most new companies do not invest the couple of days they could to really flesh these ideas out.

Operationally & Financially Speaking

63. The Cost of Goods

The foundation of the widget based business, whether the widgets are medical devices, consumer products or packaged foods, is the Cost of Goods (COG). Every decision that is made in the business is built on the fundamental knowledge of "what does it cost completely, to make one selling item".

Unique to the widget business is the fact that in order to take revenue from Customers, something tangible must be delivered. Service businesses or software/app based businesses have different models which both require different investments of time or capital to create revenue.

I've always been surprised at how often the COG is not taken seriously enough by startups and early stage businesses. Now, with the advent of crowd-sourcing, numerous entrepreneurs are finding themselves having funded the cost of a production run, but not appreciated the full COG let alone the other costs it will take to actually build a business.

This article is exclusively on the COG, and it is relatively easy to describe, but, complicated to solve. The COG encompasses all costs directly associated with acquiring the widget and being able to deliver it to a buyer. The operative words are **all costs**. Here is why:

Amanda is a baker and is planning to make organic/gluten free cookies and wants to sell them in local stores.

She's created a nice package and will sell them in boxes. Her sales unit is the box of cookies. Amanda will be making the cookies from her family recipe at a local commercial kitchen because she loves to bake.

Amanda knows how much the recipe ingredients cost that go into each box of cookies – $1.35 – and calls that her COG.

Here is what Amanda has NOT included in her COG:

Amanda buys all the ingredients from local wholesale providers. They are delivered via UPS for which she pays to have them shipped to her. Not included.

Sometimes she buys volume from a local supplier and picks them up herself. The cost of her time is not included.

Amanda puts her personal labor into the production of the cookies, which she has not quantified in hours per batch or dollars per box. Not included. (BTW – That means she is working for free.)

Amanda has waste in her process with broken cookies at some unknown percentage of each production that don't get to the box. Not included.

Amanda personally does the packaging, forms the boxes, fills and seals the bags and puts the finished boxes into cartons. Not included.

Amanda rents the time needed at the commercial kitchen on an hourly basis. Not included.

Amanda is saying in her COG of $1.35, that all other costs to produce her cookies are in fact, free. Going through this exercise with Amanda, we found her actual COG to be almost $3.50, almost triple her original thought! Her complaint that she had no money in her business to grow it, started to make a lot of sense based on the COG awareness problem. Her desire to scale up and add retail distribution instead of selling retail at farmer's markets was starting to look slim. Retailers will need to make a margin on the product, as will the eventual distributors who will sell to the retailers, which would leave Amanda in a hopeless cycle of working for free and never really understanding how this business can grow without more of her free labor.

Every conversation I have with people starts in the COG area. Is the COG comprehensive? Is it optimized (best pricing). Does the business owner know what steps can be taken to improve it (volumes necessary)? If you know these answers, you're way ahead of the curve. Simply looking at the ingredient costs or the materials costs is not enough. Take the time (an hour or two, tops) to really think through how much it costs, for all the steps associated with making your widget and getting it to you, including freight, people's time, waste, etc., and get your COG. Do it with every product you create, every time. The entire business stands literally on top of that awareness. You can't begin to envision how much you can spend on any of the other parts of your business until you know what it costs to make the products you are selling.

64. Inventory: The bank account that's not in a bank

Once you have multiple items and a flowing inventory stream, inventory becomes a very real challenge. With inventory on demand by Customers, stocks running low on different items at different rates, supply chain hiccups or delays, issues in customs, all in all, it takes on the appearance of a dynamic nightmare.

What is often lost in this process is the very real awareness that the inventory is the life-blood of the business. Every piece of inventory is worth an amount that was paid for it, and an amount for which it can be sold. Therefore, each piece of inventory carries a legacy of previously spent money, future derived revenue and a potential for profits.

Being out of stock, having overstocks, having supply problems, are all par for the course in the best run businesses. How well the business management keeps track of inventory demands, talks to their customers and suppliers, pays attention, maybe daily, to the ebb and flow of inventory is no less important to the business than it is for the stockbroker looking to buy and sell stocks watching inventory levels and price movements.

Yet, despite all of this vital importance of inventory and the money it represents, many entrepreneurs treat their inventory with low importance. For any inventory based business to thrive, however, it is inventory, and therefore the inventory management, that will make that happen.

Proper management of inventory is complicated. To manage the logistics, planning and replenishment takes a devoted effort and ongoing maintenance. Measuring inventory turns and knowing how well the money it represents is working for your business if critical, especially in the early stages of a business when every dollar counts. Whether dealing with MOQs, JIT, 3PLs or any other acronym, it is and always will be, the inventory that makes the business fly. Your inventory needs to be *just right* for your business to thrive. Anything less is costing you *opportunity AND money*. And it doesn't take a college degree to know that when you run out of opportunity or money, the business is toast.

65. Gross Margin is about dollars, not percentage

There are those that may hold a perspective that achieving certain gross margin percentages makes a business viable. There is no doubt that higher margin percentages are better than lower margin percentages. What I tend to hear though is that if XX% is achieved, all is well for the future, which, in my opinion, is entirely the wrong approach to understanding your business.

Let's spend a minute going through the math basics (sorry, if you hated math in school, but, you're running a business). If you're selling a low price item, say $10 at a 40% gross margin, that means that your COG is $6. 4 out of every 10 dollars is available for discretional expenses like marketing, overhead, paying yourself, paying sales people, etc. If you can reduce the costs to produce the item to $3 instead of the $6 it currently costs, that would mean 7 out of every 10 dollars collected goes to expenses. Clearly 70% gross margin is better than 40%.

What is truly important though, is how many dollars your company needs to become economically sustainable and how much reach your company has to get those sales.

For every 1000 transactions at $10, in the best case above at 70% Gross Margin, the company creates $7000. Awesome; maybe. Can you create 1000 transactions at $10? Does $7,000 cover everything? What if you only create 500 transactions? What if you need $10,000.

By stark contrast in a different scenario, if you are selling $50 items at 40% gross margin, to create the same $7000 of gross margin, you only need to sell 350 items. It is likely far less actual work to find 350 customers than to find 1000 customers.

There is an adage that you pay your bills with dollars and not percentages. Do the math and be really confident about how many actual TRANSACTIONS (wholesale or retail-you still need consumers) you will need to create in order to make any money in margin dollars. The easiest way to go out of business is to have lots of transactions with really high margins at really low prices, and not enough gross margin dollars to sustain the business. When someone gives you a "rule of thumb", be sure they are also telling you at what price for the products and with what overhead costs. Those are controllable numbers!

There is NO silver bullet. The savvy business person knows the numbers they are working to achieve for the outcome they seek. The percentages are like a tachometer in your car; at best a tachometer can tell you how hard your engine is working. It won't tell you how fast you're going or how soon you will achieve your destination, which is actually what you care about.

BTW, the tachometer is irrelevant enough in automobiles that many don't even have them anymore.

66. Credit: A sale is not complete until you collect the money

One of the biggest differences before a business moving from B2C to wholesale is payment terms and credit. We can all envision selling lemonade to consumers and taking cash. In wholesale, stores are issued payment terms for their payments to give them time to sell the products to even out their cash flows. How you issue credit to these companies can make or break your business. People new to business, or who come from the "online" world, are typically not well versed in the massive risk they may have in issuing credit to retailers or distributors, often providing credit to a customer just because they exist.

The terms offered to a retailer are in concept exactly like the terms American Express or Visa offer to a consumer. There is a credit amount and a mutually acceptable timed payment agreement. In consumer products that agreement opens the door to the shipment of goods to the retailer. No agreement on terms, by either party, and there is no shipment of goods to the retailer.

The dance that is the credit limit and payment terms conversation is critical to the foundation of the relationship between the two parties. Terms of net 90 (payment will be made 90 days after shipment) means the inventory put out today will not become actual cash for your company to spend on something for 3 months. If you don't have 3 months of rent, payroll, etc., already in place, you can't take the arrangement.

Once agreed to, both parties must do all in their power to meet the expectations of the other so as not to create a difference of opinion at the time payment should be due. Any hiccup in the process can derail an entire project. Particularly in the area of chargebacks.

Most people don't realize that large scale retailers now typically all have chargeback systems whereby they reserve the right to take an automatic deduction (chargeback) for any misstep the vendor may have in the transaction process. These chargebacks are now part of a menu of screw-ups that vendors over the years have inadvertently created for retailers. A late shipment costs $50 per carton. Failure to send an invoice on time costs $2500 per invoice. These are only examples. The list goes on and on.

Chargebacks will also delay a payment. Imagine a $20,000 invoice that is important to your business, being charged back (discounted) by the customer $3,500 (after the fact) for whatever reason and then not being paid on time because it is now going through additional processing at "Big Store". It can be crippling to a new or young business. Cash flows can be everything.

Having experienced our own challenges over the years, and watching retailers continue to ratchet up the number of ways they can take discounts, we have always been very tight with credit. We review businesses, call other vendors, set realistic payable credit limits and watch the payment practices over time. We read through vendor manuals for every possible glitch that might arise. Through experience with the downsides of credit and chargebacks, we protect the income as much as is possible so the final amount paid to us by the retailer equals the initial amount invoiced and it gets paid on time. No one wants to have a million dollars in sales for which they only got paid $600k. Yet, it happens, all the time.

67. What are your metrics?

Everything about growing your business is about scaling. It is easy to add 1 single store retail customer when you have lots of inventory of all the things you sell. It is an entirely different process to add 1 distributor or to add 1 chain store with 50 locations. Those kinds of blips can be upsetting (in a good way) to the supply chain or the cash flows and income streams. How you keep score as to what might represent a shaking of the tectonic plates is the management's primary responsibility. To do that, you have to KNOW what represents a mild shake from a significant earthquake (I am a Californian after all). To do that requires a personal matrix of checkpoints or "metrics" by which you can assess the health and size of your business. If a single event is going to add a 25% growth in revenue, that is pretty major. On the other hand, if all that action is coming only on 1 SKU, it may not be a very big deal at all.

My metrics have always been through watching bookings and inventory movement. Revenue alone does not describe a business. It's a leveling agent, but, does not tell enough of the story. If you have multiple products in multiple categories, knowing how your supply chains work for each category and what might represent a significant shakeup in that area is key to being able to steer growth where you can most handle it. No inventory equals no revenue in consumer products.

If Ms. Big Customer is finally willing to take in your product, and she wants the thing that is most difficult to produce or provides the smallest margins to your business, you may or may not wish to entertain that business at this time or any time. On the other hand, if you only need to make a phone call to change your supply chain from 50 every once in awhile to 500 (a ten fold increase) every month, then taking that business, perhaps at some concession like free freight, is more than worth it.

But, if you don't know your "metrics" on how much of that item you sell and how often and how the new cash flows will affect your needs in 45 or 75 days, you will lose sleep when the reality sets in later that you have committed to something that is risky or worse, that will compromise other customers or just plain can't be done.

Know how much you sell of your products in pieces and in dollars and sleep better at night. Keep score through your reports at a minimum of a monthly basis. Get down to granular levels periodically too. It's quite possible that product you created that looks like it is going to be wonderful is selling 90% of the volume to just one Customer. All of a sudden that product needs help getting spread around to other Customers. Without good insight into what's really happening, through bookings (when the order comes in), sales (when the order ships), you are pretty much piloting your ship in the fog.

Get to know your business, its costs and revenue streams better than you know your personal finances and needs. How well do you know your car or house payments? Know business numbers at least as well and then when opportunity comes knocking, you will have exactly the right awareness to make strong decisions quickly and easily without losing any sleep over the decision. That's how you grow.

68. Account Value Metrics

Over the years, I have come to deeply respect the simplicity of account value metrics. To be "sharp" at the game of growing a consumer product business, in my opinion, you have to be able to understand the actual value an account can bring to a company. To do that, I have learned (or created, I'm not sure which), the two simplest ways to achieve that awareness.

Fundamentally, adding more accounts and doors is a good thing. It expands the number of consumers who will buy the products – pretty obvious. But, which accounts are worth more than others and are therefore, harder to get into and more valuable when you do (and more protected by the existing brands in the stores)? So here are my formulas.

There are two methods I use: the **retailer's inventory turn rate** needed to keep the space or the **likely consumer purchasing method** used to determine the reorder rates needed to keep up with demand.

Here is the **Inventory Turn Rate** method: You sell one item to a store. It takes 6 of them to fill a hook or a shelf space. Those 6 items x 3 inventory turns per year is 18 sold items per year. If each item is $10 wholesale, then that space at that account is worth $180 per year in revenue to your company. You sell a collection of 10 items to the account, each at 6 per hook or a shelf space, which becomes 180 sold items per year. That account is worth $1800 per year.

The alternate way from the demand side is to do the math via purchase rate. Sales of 1 unit every week is 52 units a year. In the previous example, with only 6 on a hood, that is far greater than 3 inventory turns. At $10 per item that it $520 per year per item. Now let's apply it.

Walgreens has 9000 stores. Band aid 1" strips are in all stores. The wholesale price to Walgreens is $1 and a shelf holds 5 with inventory turns of 10 times a year (this is an illustration not a fact). That little space that the little box sits in is worth $450,000 a year ($1 x 5 x 10 x 9000) to Band Aid. That means to Walgreens, if they are going to replace that Band Aid 1" strip with something else, it is a $1 million decision (they mark it up), for one little space. Is a box a week the right sales rate? What if it is two? You need to know for your product.

It is exactly this math that gets your juices flowing, but, can also make clear why 1 tiny little product in Walgreens (or anywhere else) fails or succeeds. Fail to produce the revenue by actually selling the volume to consumers, and you're out. Fail to support the effort by bringing consumers to the space, and you're out. Fail to price the product properly and not deliver the results, and you're out. Have some other brand come in with a better offer, and you're out.

Know the math that matters to the buyer and then how you can achieve scalability AND support it. Your product at Walgreens could be a wonder product, but, failing to drive traffic and support it may lose the most precious real estate that product may ever attain. That's exactly why Walgreens is not very inclined to take on an unproven product and why Band Aid has 50 SKUs (or more) in Walgreens. Go with what you can trust. Everything else is risk.

69. Financing your growing business

There is all kinds of talk about partnerships in the market today. Generally having a partner stems from the idea that one party may have knowledge or expertise in an area the other party does not. Many times it boils down to one has money and the other does not. Maybe it is angel or venture money. Whatever it is, it always brings a new, often difficult conversation about equity.

I personally don't like to give up equity and will do all I can to avoid it. As such, over the years, I've become a fan of debt financing. In the early stages of a business, and even into the long haul, that financing needs to be based on something tangible as collateral. When you buy a house or a car, the lender can simply take your house or car and theoretically be paid back for the money they loaned.

However, often times with business growth, opportunities come along that stretch the capital of the business. 30% growth is generally fundable internally, but, 75% growth (putting 75% more money into inventory) may be beyond your reach. I once had an opportunity to sell a $200k initial program to Kmart and did not have the capital to buy the inventory at that quantity. We were running at inventory of about $75k, so a single buy of an additional $100k of inventory was a big leap. So, I found a lender at the time that would finance the Purchase Order using the collateral of the eventual Accounts Receivable as the back up for the loan. This practice is called Purchase Order Funding.

I asked my friend Carolyn McClure at Security Business Capital what some of the things were that made this type of lending productive and what were the things the Company would need to consider prior to the conversation.

First and foremost, your customers need to be credit worthy and your supply chain reliable. If the product may not perform or if your customers may not pay you, then the loan is not going to be paid back. In reality, the lender is financing your customer's ability to pay, not yours. Financing an entire portfolio of accounts receivable is a good way to generate immediate capital while not needing to change the payment terms with your customers. In a cash flow crunch, this is productive. This practice is called Invoice Factoring.

Second, your terms need to be final. In some parts of retail, product not sold after a certain period is returned to the vendor. In that case, the lender does not want the inventory, it wants the money.

Third, you need to have your books in order. Loans come much more easily to a company that has a crystal clear understanding about margins, costs, A/R, inventory on hand value, etc. and is able to produce that information in a clear, tight financial report.

Lastly, this relationship should be put together prior to the need, based on your growing business and the possible need for short term capital to get you up the ladder. You can't always get the extended payment terms from your vendors that you need to do business at larger and larger volumes. It is normal to find that your capital in the business continues to grow because of larger and larger levels of inventory. As you see this develop, get educated about what options you have BEFORE you give up equity just to get growth capital.

70. Crowdfunding is no panacea

Lots of product developers are convinced that if they do a crowdfunding campaign of some kind at Kickstarter or Indiegogo, that their golden path to success will lay itself out before them. For many that turns out to be the yellow brick road to a meeting with the Wizard of Oz, whom we all know carries no weight whatsoever.

These campaigns are at best marketing tools to get consumer or more accurately funder enthusiasm and at worst, pre-sales events that create a whole host of unexpected problems pushing on supply chains, testing the inexperience of the product developers and irritating a community of enthusiasts.

In my opinion, the best way to start a company is to "grow" it. Just as the term implies, growth happens when some small thing, a plant or a critter, goes through the stages of its life, becomes educated through those stages and becomes better capable at each subsequent stage.

What the crowdfunder is seeking is to set off an explosion, to create an immediate and significant place in the market, generally because they have been convinced that scale matters.

The U.S. did not get to the moon by starting with Apollo. By running a hyper-successful crowdfunding campaign, a product developer misses all the mistakes that can happen along the way. I can certainly hire companies or people with experience, but, few have any resources so they "wing it" thinking they can work it all out.

Newsflash: That practice causes really big problems and when those problems arise, it tends to alienate the exact people that trusted them in the first place – those early adopter funders. To most of these folk's credit, at least they do not generally become as irrelevant as vaporware, but, many come pretty close.

The best outcome for a crowdfund campaign can be to achieve exactly what the campaign design should be – enough funders and revenue to produce the initial product in the quantity that the product developer has planned. To simply add a zero to a production run is easy, but, not for the supply chain. Those issues become part of every step of production.

A campaign looking for $30,000 at an average of $50 per funder is 600 funders. The hyper-success of $300,000 is then 6000 funders! That's going to be 6000 shipments. That is going to require 6000 pieces. It is 10 times as much volume manufacturing time. It's 10 times the number of people who may become impatient because delays have happened at the factory that had committed to 1 week production but now needs 6 weeks of production time because getting parts in that volume takes longer. The list goes on and on.

As much as we all would love to simply be able to create a 10x increase in our business, you have to have a robust infrastructure to accommodate it. Sometimes 10x is spontaneous combustion that goes past the limit. At what risk are you willing to have the limits pushed to the edge and possibly compromise the very thing you set out to do?

Creating and Navigating Growth

71. When startup ends, scaling can begin

I've always presumed that any business can scale. I always presumed that any business owner would want their business to scale. In the February issue of Fast Company, there was an article from a forthcoming book by David Butler and Linda Tischler called *Design to Grow: How Coca-Cola Learned to Combine Scale and Agility* in which the authors make a case that there has been a false hope focus on starting a business and that the future of startups would be improved greatly if the focus were on scaling a business. I was particularly intrigued with how the authors have been able to distinguish between the start up phase of a business and the scaling phase, particularly the stark contrast in perspective needed in each phase.

Having done both and not realized we were doing it, I never appreciated that startup and scale do not sync. Here's the compelling excerpt from the article:

Starting is all about agility. When you're starting, you're developing assets (your IP, your product, your brand, your retail relationships).

Scaling is all about leveraging your assets to get the most value out of them.

Starting requires lots of exploration and rapid iteration to get to your business model.

Scaling is all about standardizing and executing your business model so that you can take advantage of network effects.

Starting is all about being ready to pivot when you need to—the whole team must be ready to rethink everything if things aren't working.

Scaling is all about planning—developing a core competency in planning is critical.

Finally, **starting** is all about staying lean: moving very fast while doing the most with the least amount of resources. All startups start with constrained resources, so this is almost intuitive. But big companies think big—they think in millions and years and functions, not in hundreds and weeks and individuals.

Whichever phase you are in, the future of your business is up to the choice you make between your willingness to let go of the attributes of being a startup and embracing the attributes of becoming scalable. Of course, not all businesses must become scalable. Both can be successful. One is personal, the other is scalable.

Forever startup now to me looks almost like an artisanal business. It's the tinkerer and the "always say yes" person. It's the person who wants to leave options open.

To scale is to say no, we don't do that. It is to set boundaries. It is to use systems as a framework on which to build a significantly larger business.

Hats off to every one of the half million new startups every month in the U.S.. What a shame that so many will fail before even getting to this juicy subject. How amazing that most aspire to scale but, will never achieve that because they can't figure out how to stop being a startup. That's the allure of being a startup – if you really enjoy it, or you think that is just how it needs to be, you can't make it to scalability – without help.

72. Scalability – What is it?

I have learned through experience that scalability does not have the same meaning to all business owners. There are also multiple types of scalability in a business. Knowing which scaling issues are possible for your business and how to address them before they start happening is a top priority for any business owner or manager.

Most people think of scaling as simply getting more orders or higher volumes, but, that is a simplistic view. What makes scaling a challenge is knowing what other workloads those increases in sales bring with it. In consumer products it can be many things.

Some scaling, like that of a website getting more visitors, takes no infrastructure at all and therefore requires only the awareness that the website must have increased volume capacity to be scaled. Higher volumes of sales of a tangible item are not the same though since each added item creates potentially multiple levels of human labor to complete. Products do not pick themselves off the shelf to be shipped yet.

Here is how wholesale scaling works in real life today.

Higher volumes of sales of the same thing to the same customer is pretty straightforward. One order a week for 100 pieces becomes one order a week for 200 pieces. Double the business, and the only additional work is more pieces in a box done by a contracted fulfillment company. One shipment a week. One invoice a week. One eventual payment a week.

More often the scenario in wholesale is orders of the same product to multiple customers. Now there are 10 orders a week for 100 pieces. Ten times the business.

Now there are 10 shipments a week, 10 invoices a week and eventually 10 payments a week. Ten times the work load to take in 10 times the money.

Then we have the multi-product scenario where each order has a unique assortment of items in it. Now 10 orders are each unique so the order processing is not copying the previous but in fact converting a PO of assorted items into the necessary documents to get that unique assortment of goods out of the warehouse. The shipment for each is unique. The invoices are unique. The payments though are still 10 payments. However, now the inventory demand is irregular and replenishment of the better sellers will be sooner than replenishment for the slower sellers creating future added activity. This common scenario is more than 10 times the workload.

You can't economize, human labor, be it picking products from a shelf, taking telephone calls, the preparation of orders, communication with warehouses, vendors or Customers, along with receiving payments and depositing them to a bank is all difficult to scale and they do not scale at the same rates.

Managing for the scale of a business tomorrow so that people will be in place and trained to provide the work as it comes along and as it grows, is a critical management challenge for the business owner/manager . Failing to do a good job makes the work seem overwhelming for the staff and can create quality problems as overtaxed people take on tasks with which they have limited experience. Being prepared not for today or tomorrow, but, for 3 weeks from now is the difference between playing for the long term or playing to keep up or maybe incrementally ahead of the workload. It's not easy, but, what is easy can be done by anyone.

73. The three ways to grow your business

Many small companies get very good at solving problems. As a result, they are great at "how". It is easy to get very caught up in the how because it moves toward a solution and feels really good. Often though, businesses will start down the "how" path without having truly identified the who, what, when, where and particularly the why first. There is a reason in business anyway, that "how" comes at the end of who, what, when, where, why and how. So this is the oversimplified starting point when trying to consider how to grow your business.

Fundamentally, there are only three ways to grow your business. All growth strategies come back to one of these basic building blocks. This makes planning for your growth straight-forward enough, but, it does not make it easy. Having some plan, even a bad plan, is better than no plan at all. Here are the three ways to grow your business and some considerations along the way.

Get more money per item you sell. Provided you have no drop off of customers or slow down of sales activity, you can grow your business by raising your prices or selling pricier stuff. Of course you have market conditions (i.e. competition) that may negate this option or make it unreasonable, in which case you will need to visit the second and third ways.

Sell more stuff to the people you already know. Your Customers can always be asked to buy more volume. You can work harder to sell everything you can to your Customers. You can also expand your product range to have more things to sell. In the end, this strategy is expanding annual revenue produced by the existing Customers. It is this strategy that typically drives new product development initiatives. Sales costs are low. Marketing costs are low. Product development costs generally are high.

Sell your existing stuff to a broader audience. The folks you don't know yet could buy your stuff, too. You could do more trade shows? You could do more e-mailings? You could hire more sales people and they could sell your stuff to the people they know? Sales costs will be high. Marketing costs are high. Product development costs are low.

To create a plan for success, look at these three areas individually and develop a strategy for each one that you want to pursue. Always look at how you can raise your prices. Always consider how you can sell more things to the same Customers. Always consider how to develop new relationships.

In doing the planning, be sure to include target expectations, with time and resource definitions and a calendar. Some things will work. Some will not. If you don't understand what game you are playing, you can't keep score. Only through score keeping can you determine what is performing better and what is not.

If your business is small, identify an amount of money you wish to come out of pocket to invest. Be aware that some things, like sales investments are mostly your time since the payments will come only on the successful sales. Others like product development may only be your personal time. While still others, like trade shows are your money and your time. If you put all your time in one area, you won't have the time you need to achieve one of your other objectives. The same is true with your money. Spend them both wisely.

One of the arts of business is determining what portion of your limited resources (time or money) is the appropriate portion to devote to your growth. Once you determine what amount of resources it will be overall, then you portion it again toward each of the above mentioned three areas. Then, hold yourself accountable with ongoing monitoring via the scorekeeping.

Once you know what works better and what does not work, it gets even more fun – was it what you did, or was it how you did it? Isn't the art of business great!!!

74. When is it time to create new products?

Too many companies jump on new products far too early largely because retailers always ask "what's new". That is the retailer's habit, not their need. In the rush to new products, companies work under the belief that the 12 month calendar equals the amount of time it takes their actual company to fully market a product. The reality is few early stage companies have the sales system in place to saturate their audience with the products they already have, let alone introduce new ones.

Step back and take this vantage point: if you have 200 doors now and you want to add 200 more doors, the new ones have not carried or likely even seen any of what is currently being sold. Therefore, what is old to you is ALL new to them. Getting the 200 new doors is MORE valuable than creating new products for an under-developed sales channel. You likely do not even need new products. What you need is more thorough selling efforts with your existing products. New for new sake is not a strategy, it's a waste of money and time, your time.

Always know where you want to go, why you want to go there and particularly what it will take to get there. Your company is not a collection of products. It is a collection of systems by which related products can be brought to market to grow the business. If your sales system is hap hazard, spend the time developing it into an organization.

Focus on the systems (not the products) to figure out the best products you need to develop to grow. Every new product is a distraction to selling the existing products. Don't introduce new until there is so much demand for it that when you do it, it is truly game changing. Your company value is in the systems it has developed that are effective. They are the veins and arteries of your company's life. Your products fill the veins and arteries. Growth comes from extending the veins and arteries or making them able to carry more volume.

Focus on being good at selling what you have (your selling system) before you entertain investing in new products. Then, take any new ideas through a thorough systems approach to compare and contrast different ideas to find the best options for where your business is at that time and where you want to get to from there.

75. What to think about when you consider new products

You've created some productive products. You have a sizable percentage or quantity of your target audience carrying the products and they are selling through in those stores. You have a consumer following of people who care about what you do or make. You have a sales force that can deliver whatever you come up with to the retailer audience so that your efforts in developing the new products are not a waste of time. You have a presence at trade shows that makes your products shine and attracts your existing customers and new ones to your space at any show you do. It's time to look at something new.

I am a firm believer in a systemic approach to the process, informed by any kind of market awareness. At the earliest possible stage evaluate new products with the inclusion of market awareness of the number of existing stores that would likely carry the new products, how much getting to new stores might cost in time and resources (perhaps new shows, new sales people, etc.) and eventually the sales and gross margin contribution potential for each investment.

Let's take a hypothetical example; a healthy energy bar has 5 flavors and wants to consider how to grow their business. After 3 years, the business has 800 doors carrying at least 3 of the 5 flavors. The product is available through outdoor stores (REI, etc.), natural food stores (Whole Foods, etc.) and assorted other locations where people who are health conscious and active shop.

To establish their focus on the future, they need to determine a new nexus of health conscious consumers that are active, the internal capabilities of their company and the retail channels they are in, or aspire to be in to grow their business.

They could easily expand to another couple of flavors, which could expand their existing real estate. They could create new packaging or new marketing efforts to find other retail locations that might be productive like college stores or airport stores. Both of these are inexpensive. A great place to start.

They could go into energy drinks, which could be sold to both of the existing channels, is still a consumable but might need to meet new buyers although not new stores. They may not have any expertise in energy drinks, so the development might be time consuming.

They could modify their energy bar recipe to make it into a granola recipe and go after a deeper penetration into the Natural Food business. That would not extend the Outdoor store market and would also require the establishment of the brand as a healthy breakfast product for more every day consumption. Their existing supply chain may be able to do this reducing the development costs.

They could create a multipack of some sort, which would extend their real estate but likely not their audience.

They could look at their retail or consumer audience and find a niche to develop something completely different like performance apparel for example. That would likely not expand the natural food store business, but could get it into more apparel oriented locations, but, they have no relationships there, so it will be time consuming and expensive in resource commitment. This also would begin to transform the business from a consumables to a durables business and require an entirely new supply chain. Another resource depleting effort.

Depending on the 3-5 year desires and the resource commitments and expected revenue streams these ideas and more would be considered prior to going down any specific path. The more disciplined and thoughtful the evaluation, the more likely the company is to create products that are meaningful to their customers and meaningful to their business.

76. When the market is slow to adopt your product, then what?

This question haunts many. Rarely in consumer products does a new product light up the bank accounts in the first weeks of being available to the market. There are lots of reasons for a market to be slow to adopt and lots of things you can do. Before you just start deploying tactic after tactic to make your efforts work out consider where all your ideas thus far have come from – YOU. Since you have spent the last months focused on getting your product out there, what you need to get at this moment is a heavy dose of outside thinking.

You need to make contact with everyone you have met and crossed paths with in your journey thus far and talk it out. The observations and opinions of that collective constitutes your personal library of ideas outside your four walls. With the combined value of the dozens (or more) of years of either doing what you do or working with others who did what you are doing, you can gain a broad range of insights to consider to change the direction of your efforts, or maybe just encourage you to be more patient. You need ideas. You need outsider perspective and you need it fast to put some wind in your sails.

Who are these people?

Your vendors and service providers are a good starting point. Your 3PL, your accountant, the people who make what you sell, the people who make your packaging have all worked with lots of companies with this challenge. Ask them what they think of your efforts and results thus far.

Your sales people are a second place (provided you have contracted some, if not that is likely the first tactic you may want to consider). Sales people have all had multiple brands that were slow out of the blocks and turned into revenue producers for them.

Your advisors and consumer product contemporaries are another resource. Maybe you met others at a trade show or trade event. Any existing business has had product introductions go slowly. Find out why and what their response was.

Maybe Meetup or Linked in or some other online community has connected you to other consumer product company business owners.

Your retail customers, the ones you have gotten to prove the concept would be delighted to spend 20 minutes with you offering their ideas of how to move forward. Your problem is getting sell through in stores or adding more stores, not the product itself.

The point is when the going gets tough, and it always does, is exactly the time to reach out to your network and get ideas. The inclination is to close the blinds and work harder. Resist. Instead listen to stories. In fact, what you need is an assortment of different points of view. You need the benefit of experience that is different from yours. You won't really get new perspectives from the same person who provided the current point of view – YOU. Reach out. Admit the challenge you face and make adjustments. Maybe all you need to be is more patient.

Effective and Efficient Time Savers

77. The item number

Some people have a tendency to try to overthink the creation of product item numbers (a SKU # or Stock Keeping Unit) working to create elaborate systems that only make the usefulness of the number more difficult. The item number is the shorthand code for the unique identity of the product and should therefore be in the shortest and easiest way possible to uniquely identify any product you make.

Everyone from your customers, to your vendors, to your website, to your sales people, to the reports you create will be driven by item numbers and the item number sort. It is critical to think SIMPLIFY so that it becomes useful to you and to all the others that will be handling (and making money from) your product.

These are our recommendations.

- Don't use hyphens, dashes or other non-alphanumeric elements. It can confuse uploads and transfers and wastes character spacing.

- Make all your item numbers the same length, generally 5-8 digits/characters.

- Numbers are far better than characters. Unless you need a digit position with 26 variables instead of 10, stick exclusively with numbers. (BTW, if you must use letters, don't use the ones that might look like a number, like O, Q or lower case L).

- If you must use letters, don't try to use letters that mean something. BLU and BLK or XS and XL is cumbersome. A=Black and B=Blue, 2=extra small and 7= extra large, and then fit the other sizes or colors in range. Assign the letters and numbers and don't try to make them descriptive. Simpler is better.

- If you want category, product, size, color, work from left to right to get your final SKU #.

- Always keep in mind the item number is the organizing tool that all the warehouses or data bases your product ever finds itself in will be used to keep it organized for location. (Remember the Dewey decimal system and the library?) If you put letters in the middle, they will be sorted as such. If you want all your groupings of similar products of every size and color in the same place in a report, then keep the variables of size and color on the far right.

- Don't waste digits that can be reused after a couple of years off. Two digits for color suggests that the product may have 99 colors. If you only have 2 or 3 at a time, you can always recycle unused numbers in a couple of years (depending on your business). There are simple ways to make numbers work as category identifiers.

Your SKU#s are NOT the UPC numbers. Those are not important to codify in any way. Learn your item numbers well. Everyone who buys, sells and handles your products will be looking at reports of the sales of these items. This is all that matters to everyone; the quantity sold, on order or on hand and the item number. Everything else only matters to the consumer.

78. Image management

If you're in the consumer product world, the BEST thing that can happen is to have lots of people use your photos without needing to hunt you down or ask your permission. That means the best place to keep your library of photos is in some public place where people can download the best images you have produced; the cloud, with no bank vault with passwords.

Take the time now to build a library with referencing, product identification, by item number, properly spelled names, etc., for any blogger, retailer or casual looker to find in your "photo albums". And then leave them there. There is nothing more time consuming or frustrating than hunting for images on your hard drive, your server or your phone when someone "needs" it.

Whether they are product shots, logos, lifestyle shots, fun pictures, whatever, if they are associated with product already in the market place, the more public the better. Your competitors can already go buy your product, so get over competition. If you control the original content and make it accessible from your website, through links, not to mention from the cloud site itself (like Flickr or Picassa, not Facebook), you are far less likely to have crappy images all over the landscape that do not show off what you want to have shown off as well as you can. Your branded images will also enhance the visits in all the places they go. Everything is one Google search or one click away for your brand. Cross linking these online sites also helps SEO.

This one step, started when your library is small, can save you and your team (sales people, marketing, etc.) hundreds of hours a year. Don't wait to do filing until some point when filing is arduous. Be smarter than the competition. Do it now. Then put the link on your website, your email signatures, etc. Life just got easier.

79. Email controls

A lot of startup business owners try to consolidate all their correspondences in one place for convenience and then answer them all, all the time. The truth is that is not scalable. Here is how to create a scalable email effort.

First, don't offer the same email address to all your contacts or bring all your communications from your marketing efforts to the same address. You want to build a self-sorting system of connections that can be managed by you or others as your business requires as it grows. Create lots of email addresses with non-name identities and when you or whomever responds, use that address as the return address.

Orders@ This is pretty obvious. Whomever in your company is your transaction person gets these. This discrete email box gets checked once or twice daily. NO MORE. Maybe you put an auto-responder on it to thank the sender somehow and tell them what will happen next and the timeframe in which that will happen.

Info@, Service@, Inquire@, media@. These and many other possibilities are what you put on the general materials or the website for different types of activities. These addresses DO NOT FEED into your personal daily email stream. These email boxes will be addressed as a project every two or three days or as volume dictates based on importance. Real opportunities may get forwarded to your personal email address, otherwise, respond with the address to which the email was sent.

Your personal email address. This address is your cherished close and/or important relationships address. Vendor execs. Sales people. Important business contacts. It is the highest priority in your email correspondence triage. You check this multiple times a day for whatever may be important. Nothing in this box should ever be urgent.

IMPORTANT NOTE- Do not treat email as a real time tool. Turn off the auto sound feature. Turn off the interrupt everything else feature. An email box is a mailbox. You go there when you choose to go there. You don't put an alarm on the box so that it interrupts what you are actually doing with something that is unknown potentially interrupting or distracting you. Allowing email to be a distraction is the equivalent of working at a Customer Service Center just waiting for the next call. Email is a terrible tool for real time communication. When you need that, pick up the phone.

Your time will disappear like sand in an hourglass if you don't get these addresses all lined up. If you already have an overloaded personal email box, create a new one. Then notify only the important people about it. Then use an auto-responder to tell senders to your old email box that you only monitor it every few days. Be very thoughtful about the responding email addresses you provide, because that determines where returns arrive. Push inbound email to higher or lower levels by forwarding it to a different box before you respond and changing the return address.

Build a system that will suit you for the future. What you've done already was fine at the time, now you have a new perspective and can see how you can silo email to the benefit of your time management. Be smarter than the competition. Do it now. Then put the emails on your website, your signatures, etc. Life just got easier.

80. Make buying from you and your sales people easier

When you go to a new restaurant do you ever ask the waitress what she recommends or what the best sellers are? And when you do, does she have an answer?

A lot of brands are unprepared to communicate simplicity to retailers. Why, because it's easier to simply produce a catalog.

The smart restaurateurs train their wait staff to know what the best sellers are and what the recommended offer should be, because this is what is the very most likely to make the new guest happy with their first experience. Those dishes are not necessarily better than the others, they are just far more likely to create loyalty by the customer because they will provide a proven positive experience.

Loyalty from a retailer comes from your product selling through their store. Simple as that. An empty shelf gets refilled.

Looking at your business, make sure your sales materials and sales people have these elements (tools) at their disposal all the time:

1. All items in your catalog and online have item numbers listed (not UPC numbers, they are too long).

2. Items that are newer are called out from the ones that are older assisting existing customers to find what they may wish to refresh the merchandise statement.

3. Organize your catalog and price list so that it is easy to cross reference.

4. Give your sales people a list of the top sellers in each of the categories in which you classify your products. (Do you know your best sellers in each category?)

5. Give your sales people 3 opening order assortments. One at your buyer's likely comfort dollar value, one at the average value that will make for a good merchandise statement and one at a strong volume for the retailer that is totally committed to your products (depending on your price points).

6. Give your sales people photos or samples of the instore signage or other store photos that will allow the retailer to envision the presentation in their store that will create the "sell through" needed to succeed.

7. Provide an order form – even if no one uses it. It's a guide and a Call to Action. Be sure it contains any specific terms of doing business with your company.

Next time you're in a successful restaurant that attracts new customers all the time, look at their communication systems and think of your sales process. What else can you do to make it easier and easier to buy your products?

The winner of shelf space is generally not the coolest product, it is the one with the best communication tools for the salespeople to remain engaged with the retailers and consumers. The higher level of trust goes to the brands that communicate well. Make sales easier or you surely make sales harder.

About the Author

Over my life, I have always tended to make the why not decision, time after time. The first time I can remember making a why not choice was my first week of high school. I attended the meeting of the school soccer team, just to see. This was in an era before there were youth soccer leagues, soccer gear stores and soccer fields everywhere. I went to the meeting never having actually played soccer, but, was pretty good at kickball. Is that enough?

That choice worked out well for me, earning me recognitions and getting me an opportunity to attend UC Berkeley as a walk on goalkeeper a few years later. My choices in classes, majors in school and the jobs I took after I graduated were often "just to see if it was interesting" (a variant on "why not").

Having spent almost 30 years on the wholesale side of branded consumer products, as a marketer, seller, product developer and brand owner, I have developed a fascination and affinity for the entire process. There are not many "industries" where the product changes regularly, the competitors are everywhere, getting into a Customer's business is not forever and consumer shopping behavior is always changing. Consumer products is perhaps the most dynamic environment in which someone can work.

However, as much as the consumer products business is exciting, what I have learned is the art of running a business. I have used the principals, the ways of seeing, the choices of approach to fine tune a keen awareness of deliberate choice making toward the business we wanted to create at the time.

Including the years I spent selling lighting equipment to retailers to precede my leap into selling products for the shelves, I was an active participant in the beginnings of multiple technology status quo transformations. I was at the beginning of screw in fluorescent lightbulbs, motion sensing light switches, the advent of color dot matrix printing, the evolution from desktop computers to laptops, the car phone to mobile phone revolution and the shift in textiles to eco-friendly materials. We now take all of these technologies for granted in our every day life, but, at one time, it took real convincing to get buyers or consumers to accept the change that they could make.

I have always felt that if one applied a disciplined, thoughtful approach to a subject, they could learn it and find the navigation paths that would lead them to where they wanted to be. Learning to identify and apply principals and habits to your efforts to create ongoing consistency in what you do is paramount to success.

Business and life are both an art. Understanding principals and applying practice creates experience from which one improves. Just practice only creates skills, not the insights as to what alternatives might have provided a more personally satisfying outcome.

For many this book will articulate many principals they may already use, but, never thought much about. For others there may be insights that will lead to significant observations about oneself, one's work or one's success. For those people I cheer you forward all the more. I am still learning more about myself. I encourage everyone to never stop looking inward as well as outward. The one thing we CAN control in life is ourselves. Knowing how to do that is a lifelong process as we each evolve through our own experiences, desires and capabilities.

Tom

Tom
~~Hello~~@LifeOffBalance.com

Sonoma County, California

45836334R00061

Made in the USA
San Bernardino, CA
18 February 2017